PRAISE
LOVING G

M000268594

"What's the life of a family caregiver like? Only a person who has experienced the highs and many lows of being in that role can truly describe that experience. Ruth honestly shares her life and that of her husband in the long and difficult journey of living with dementia and being a family caregiver. As I was reading the very personal account of Ruth's story, I felt like I was right there with her. She makes the challenges of this caregiving journey come alive."

—Sharon Lewis, RN, PhD, FAAN, President and Developer
Stress-Busting Program for Family Caregivers

"A tribute to a touching love story, Loving Gordon gives us an authentic look inside the heart of dementia. This caregiver's narrative dives deep into the realities of how dementia affects the mind, body, and spirit of the patient, but even more so, how it impacts the people they love. Just when you wonder how one can survive such loss, Ruth Pollard will answer this question and bring you far beyond it, with the realization that love can transcend any illness or circumstance."

—Chloe Rachel Gallaway, Author
The Soulful Child: Twelve Years in the Wilderness

"Ruth Pollard's beautifully written book describes the challenges of those caring for a spouse with dementia. She shows the humanity and maturity they need to succeed in this role. She also shares how she managed her husband's care by seeking education, support, and help. Most importantly, she helps readers understand that life's most difficult experiences can deepen the soul of those who can love others. As a friend of Ruth's and a former caregiver for a spouse with dementia, I was always inspired by her."

—Jan Kilby, Writing Consultant and Freelance Writer

LOVING GORDON

A

Dementia
Caregiver's
Journey

1/15/19

Lisa, Thank you for
purchasing my book! I hope
you learn from it. It has been
a labor of love for me.

Ruth Baird Pollard

LOVING GORDON

A
Dementia
Caregiver's
Journey

RUTH BAIRD POLLARD

Editing by Carol White • Cover design by Rolf Busch • Cover photo by John Pollard
Author Photo by Kim Jew • Flourish designed by Alvaro Cabrera / Freepik

Library of Congress Cataloging-in-Publication Data
Pollard, Ruth Baird
Loving Gordon: A Dementia Caregiver's Journey
p. cm.
Paperback ISBN: 978-1-947708-32-7 • Ebook ISBN: 978-1-947708-35-8
Library of Congress Control Number: 2018965038
First Edition, December 2018

 CITRINE PUBLISHING
Asheville, North Carolina, U.S.A.
(828) 585 - 7030 • www.CitrinePublishing.com

For Annabelle, our family,
and caregivers everywhere

In Memoriam

Claude Pollard

Gordon Pollard

Kent Johansson

and

Tammy Pollard Johansson

TABLE OF CONTENTS

PROLOGUE

FALL 2017

IN MY DREAM TODAY, I heard Gordon doing some chores.

"What was in that small cardboard box out in the garage?" he wondered aloud.

"It was a ceramic egg poacher that I ordered from a friend of mine," I replied.

"Oh, so you just drop an egg in there and microwave it?" he said.

"Well, you have to put a little water in with it," I said.

He was wandering around carrying a large sheet of plastic.

"I think I can fix the box with this," he said as he walked toward the couch where I was napping.

"Come here so I can give you a kiss," I said.

He stepped toward me and leaned down. I lifted my head toward him; it felt like lead but I wanted so badly to kiss him. With great effort my lips touched his face. I could feel the rough stubble of his beard. His skin tasted slightly salty and damp. His warm cheek yielded to my gentle kiss.

I awoke thinking, *"He was so real, so real."*

As I gradually took in my surroundings and realized Gordon wasn't there, I felt sadness. He had come to me in my dream, bringing me the wonderful memory of our love.

For about five years I have dreamt of telling my family and other caregivers about Gordon's and my journey through dementia. I've yearned to share how two people navigated this difficult journey, not always perfectly but with perseverance and love—and to let them know that if we could do it, they can too. I've wanted to share how he came to the end of his earthly journey, and was made perfect and whole once again.

I arrived at the end of our path a little battered and bruised, but with a renewed purpose in life. I invite you into our world. May the story of our journey renew you and give you hope.

EXTRAVAGANT LOVE

April 13, 2011

THIS EVENING AT CHURCH the homily was about extravagant love, the kind of love demonstrated by the poor woman who saved a whole year's wages to buy an expensive oil to anoint Jesus's body after the crucifixion. The kind of love that asks for nothing in return, that gives unconditionally from an open and loving heart. At the end of the homily, our pastor asked us to think of ways we could love extravagantly, so I have started my journal again to pay tribute to Gordon; to leave something to mark our journey; to record my thoughts and feelings; to leave a record for our children and grandchildren. Unless one lives with dementia, and comes to know intimately its ravaging effects on the mind and body, it is hard to understand the effect not only on the patient, but also on the extended family as well.

People ask how I cope with everything; they say it must be awful to see the effects of dementia on Gordon, and they are right.

There are several answers. First is my abiding faith in God. Looking through the lens of my life, I can clearly see that God had prepared me for this journey. Without His preparation, I would be lost.

The second answer is that I fully accepted the fact of Gordon's dementia, almost from the day he was diagnosed. I have not denied his illness nor asked why this was happening to us. I have accepted the fact that this is simply what happened and do not ask the unanswerable question of "why?" It just is.

Thirdly, I made it a priority to become educated about dementia. There are many excellent books on the subject and the Alzheimer's Association is a wonderful resource. Also, I have as much help as possible. This is a journey one cannot undertake alone without seriously damaging one's own mental and physical health. It is vitally important to seek support from family, friends, and a caregiver support group. Many people are going through the same thing I am (and some situations are much worse). It is so helpful to talk through problems and to obtain insight from other families.

I could not stop thinking and planning for my life after Gordon. In some ways I was ready to be done with this part of our journey, yet I cherished every hour we had together. Each moment was more precious than it would have been without his dementia. In a perverse way, dementia taught me to value every moment of life. I have learned loving compassion and extreme patience. Recently, I was thinking of my future when Gordon walked into the room. I gave him a long hug and felt a twinge of guilt for planning my life when he was still there before me, his body warm, and his touch gentle.

I kissed his neck and thought, "Please forgive me for planning to go on without you."

A Love Letter

Dec 29, 2016

Dear Gordon,

People ask me why I want to write a book about living with and loving a man who has dementia. I tell them I loved you before dementia, I loved you during your years with dementia and I still love you five years after your death. I have discovered that illness and death did not diminish my love for you, but in many ways our love was enhanced. That's why I want to tell our story—to let others know that love can flourish and grow even under the clouds and fog of dementia. My book will be a gift from both of us to our families and others and maybe I can get you back a little, if only in my memory.

I remember the first time I saw you walking past my desk at work. My first thought was "Who is that?" You were so good-looking and your dark beard enhanced your warm, brown eyes and wide smile, and your relaxed manner and easy gait attracted me. It was your first day at work, about 1981. We were just friends at first; you were still married. We hung out with friends after work playing volleyball and grabbing an occasional beer. A group of us liked to go out to lunch for Mexican food about once a week. One day you made a remark about your wife that caused me to ask, "You mean she isn't the love of your life?"

You responded, "Not exactly."

I replied, "That's too bad" and wondered why a man as nice as you didn't have a happy marriage. A few months later I found out you and your second wife had divorced.

We started dating in the fall of 1983. You belonged to the theatre group where we worked. You had the role of the leading man in a British murder mystery. You said you wanted to keep things light between us because the play took up a lot of your time and concentration. However, as soon as the play was over, we wanted to spend as much time together as possible. We worked for the same company and our offices were right around the corner from each other. I told you I didn't want you hanging around my desk because I knew I would never get any work done. I wanted to keep our working and personal relationships separate.

One day we were all instructed to evacuate our building because of a gas leak. I didn't see you outside and was expressing concern to some of my co-workers. One friend said, "Why are you so concerned about Gordon?" Oops, I think I let the cat out of the bag sooner than I had intended.

I always felt entirely comfortable with you, a feeling I had never before experienced with a man. Just holding hands with you felt soft and right. We could talk for hours about any topic, except politics. Our bodies fit together so perfectly on the dance floor. A deejay once remarked, "That couple on the dance floor seems so in love." We parted reluctantly at the end of an evening. We always wanted to spend more time together, but neither of us wanted to live together before we married. We felt the commitment of marriage was important and that it would set a good example for our six kids, who were teenagers at the time.

You proposed to me on New Year's Day, 1984, and I said an enthusiastic yes. (Don't tell anybody, but you proposed in bed after a passionate session of love making!) We were married on March 31, 1984, at the Methodist Church in Lytle, Texas.

You kept a scrapbook during the months we were courting. I still have it and took it out to help me remember what we were like during that first flush of new love. You wrote me a little note that said "I owe you a penny and a lifetime of love." I don't remember if you ever paid me the penny, but you certainly gave me your lifetime of love.

So my love, this book is written to pay tribute to you and the valiant and brave way you accepted your illness and death. I pray our story will be an inspiration to others who are facing a similar journey, and hope they understand that even under very difficult circumstances, love can flourish and grow.

Loving you forever,
Ruth

2007

SUMMER 2007

JULY

ONE HOT SATURDAY AFTERNOON in the summer of 2007, Gordon put on his brown work boots, jeans, T-shirt, and straw hat and got on his blue Ford tractor to shred the front five acres of our fifteen-acre "homestead" about twenty miles southwest of San Antonio, Texas. I was inside the house that we designed and built twenty-three years beforehand, working on our computer. I could hear the comfortable sound of the tractor motor as Gordon went around and around the acreage. I liked hearing the sound; I'd grown up on a farm and often heard my dad out on his tractor. There is something appealing about a man on a tractor in a straw hat and work boots. Newly mown grass looks and smells so good. It was a perfect Saturday afternoon.

After about thirty minutes, Gordon came into the house, back to the room where I was working, and sat down on the couch. One look at his frightened, tear-stained face told me he was upset. This was a man who kept his emotions in check.

"Gordon, what's the matter?" I asked.

He said, "I was outside playing catch with Tim and when I looked around, he wasn't there. I've been driving all over looking for him."

I was stunned. His words left me breathless; his son Tim was stationed in Africa with the Marine Corps and we hadn't seen him for months. I sat beside Gordon and took his hand.

"Gordon," I said gently, "Tim is stationed in Africa. He wasn't outside with you." Gordon seemed relieved, but we both knew something was very wrong. "We need to make an appointment with Dr. Peters next week," I told him, and he readily agreed. "Has this kind of thing happened to you before?" I asked. "No," he replied, "this is the first time." Unfortunately, this hallucination wouldn't be his last.

At Gordon's appointment the next week, we both went into the small, rather sterile examination room and I observed as Dr. Peters administered the MMSE (Mini-Mental State Exam), a series of questions that health professionals use to gauge a patient's everyday mental skills, as well as their orientation as to time, place and date, to determine the presence of dementia. In two of the questions, Gordon was asked to remember the names of three common items and recall them again several minutes later. He was also asked to draw the face of a clock, with all the numerals in their correct positions and the arms indicating a specific time. He recalled the three common names, but he could not draw the clock correctly. I was both surprised and disturbed as Gordon was always so precise with his tasks. After Dr. Peters' examination, he told us he thought Gordon had Alzheimer's disease, but wanted him to get further neurological testing. We were both stunned into silence. We were starting a journey we never expected to take.

FALL 2007

OCTOBER

October 31, 2007

Click, click, click WOKE me up early one morning. Gordon was not in bed, so I got up to investigate the sound. He was in our closet holding one of his unloaded rifles, pulling the trigger over and over.

"Gordon, what are you doing?" I asked.

"I thought I heard a noise in the house, and I want to investigate," he said.

I was terrified by his actions and immediately realized I had to get the guns out of our home. "Gordon, let's walk through the house and check things out."

Nothing was amiss.

Then he said something even more terrifying. "If I have this disease, I might as well go out and shoot myself."

"Oh, Gordon, we'll get through it somehow," I said, placing my hand on his shoulder. "Come back to bed and take a nap, it's been a rough morning." Thankfully, he went back to sleep.

I retrieved the two rifles from the closet, hid them under my long pink bathrobe, tiptoed into the garage and put them in the trunk of the Honda. When I returned to the bedroom, I noticed a box of bullets on the closet shelf, so I snuck back and put them in the trunk with the guns.

It was a work day but I *knew* I had to make sure the guns were in a safe place. I called the Castroville Chamber of Commerce, where I worked as the office manager, to tell my office mate, Sharron, what was going on and that I wouldn't be coming to work.

"Do you know where I can take Gordon's guns?" I asked.

"Yes, my husband, Tom, has a gun safe at the house," she said. "You can bring them there. He should be home in about an hour."

Gordon was still sleeping, so I dressed and drove into Castroville. While waiting for Tom, I went to my church, needing to talk to someone. I thought our pastor would be there. As soon as I drove in I saw my good friends, Hal and Ruth, who were there to work in the pumpkin patch for our yearly fall fundraiser.

I poured out my heart telling them of Gordon's diagnosis and the incident of that morning. They were kind and understanding. Hal is a retired minister and Ruth is a retired nurse. They both suggested that I call Gordon's doctor and report to him what happened, which I did. He wasn't available, so I left an urgent message for him to call me.

While waiting for the doctor's return call, I drove to Tom's house and explained what had occurred. Tom and Gordon had worked together several years ago and had remained friends. Without hesitation, he took the guns and locked them and the bullets in his safe. I breathed a huge sigh of relief.

After I returned to the car, Gordon's doctor called me and I told the story once more. "You need to take him to the emergency room as soon as you can because Gordon made a suicide statement!" were his exact words.

When I returned home, Gordon was up and getting dressed.

"I was worried about you this morning, Gordon, so I called Dr. Peters and told him what happened. He wants you to go the emergency room, but let's have breakfast first." He readily agreed and we ate a peaceful breakfast of cereal with sliced bananas and toast.

When we arrived at the emergency room, Gordon was still calm and could relay in detail what had happened. The intake nurse asked him about the suicide statement. Even though Gordon responded that he would never do that, the nurse suggested Gordon be admitted to the psychiatric unit for a complete evaluation and we agreed. I drove home alone in a state of utter exhaustion. My body was sapped of energy and my mind was numb, processing the events of this day.

He was hospitalized for four or five days, being thoroughly evaluated. When I visited him, he was calm and in a good mood, as if he was on vacation in a nice hotel. Imagine that! He introduced me to his psychiatrist and some of the other patients he had befriended. Before Gordon was discharged, his doctor confirmed the Alzheimer's disease diagnosis. Much later he was diagnosed with Lewy body dementia.

My beautiful husband would never be the same.

2008

Spring 2008

April

April 7, 2008

It was gordon's sixty-seventh birthday. The next day, we'd be leaving for a trip to Dayton, Ohio, to visit Gordon's oldest son, Tim, who is stationed there with the Marine Corps, his wife, Sharon, and their two young children, Matthew and Kristina. Gordon said he needed a new pair of shoes as he showed me the worn soles.

"Why have you waited until the day before our trip to tell me you needed new shoes?" I asked. "We don't have time to buy new shoes now, so you'll have to wear those or your tennis shoes."

He wore his old shoes, but he was not happy about it.

When we returned from our Ohio trip, he again reminded me that he needed new shoes, so we drove into San Antonio to a huge big box store with countless boxes of shoes stacked up to the ceiling. Eventually he found a pair that he liked; we paid for them and drove home. But once we arrived, he tried them on again and decided he didn't like them after all.

The next day we drove back to the store to return them. I decided that we weren't going to buy another pair at the big box store because it was too big and confusing for him and too stressful for me. We approached a sales clerk with the shoes and I told her we wanted to return them, but Gordon said, "No, we need to pay for them."

"We paid for them yesterday Gordon, and today we are returning them because they weren't comfortable," I explained.

He argued for a minute or so and the sales clerk was looking very confused.

Finally I put my foot down. "Gordon, we are returning these shoes!" I said. "We will buy another pair later."

The clerk completed the return and Gordon and I returned to our car. He was as frustrated as I was full of anger.

How did my bright and logical husband become so confused?

Summer 2008

July

July 2, 2008

W E SPENT A TYPICAL day going to the doctor, this time for an MRI and X-rays of Gordon's back. After the appointment, we ate Indian food, and took in a movie, but we were both tired and kept falling asleep. We returned to his doctor's office to pick up a prescription for Namenda. On the way, Gordon suggested we stop for coffee, but since it was already 4:30 and the doctor's office closed at 5:00, I replied that we didn't have time. He saw a hardware store and wanted to stop. "We'll go to the local hardware store on Friday," I said.

His idea for coffee sounded good, so after we picked up the prescription, we drove to Castroville and stopped at Sammy's Café for pie and coffee. After we finished eating and approached the cashier to pay the eleven dollar tab, Gordon took out a five dollar bill and asked for five one's. He wanted to leave a tip on the table, something he'd recently started doing because figuring out the tip and adding it to the total amount on the debit slip had become difficult for him.

When the cashier gave him his change, he put it in his wallet. As the cashier waited, I asked Gordon if he wanted to pay the tab on his debit card. He said no, so I took out my debit card. The cashier processed the tab and put the debit slip on the counter. Gordon started to sign it, but I gently took his hand, saying I should sign it because it was my debit card. I asked if he wanted to put the tip on our table, but he replied, "I already left it."

I became impatient. "You did not leave the tip," I said, taking a dollar from his hand to give to our waitress.

When we left, Gordon was upset. "You are no help to me, you only make the situation worse," he said, "and you can't keep things straight anymore." He went on to insist that he gave the cashier a ten dollar bill and a five.

"You did not," I argued, strongly assuring him that I was just trying to keep him from being embarrassed.

"I am not embarrassed," he said.

"What should I do in these situations then?" I asked.

"Just wait and if you see a problem, *then* step in," he said.

I told him that is what I did. I had yet to learn how fruitless it is to argue with a person who has dementia. We rode home in silence.

"Can we kiss and make up?" I asked after I'd parked the car in the garage and turned off the ignition.

He didn't respond.

When we entered the kitchen, I took my cell phone out of my purse and turned it on. Within a few seconds, I heard the ring tone notifying me that I had a message. I called my voicemail—it was my daughter-in-law, Sibylle, telling my fourteen-month-old granddaughter to say "hi" to Grammie Ruth. Then I heard a tiny voice saying, "hi, hi, hi!" I marveled for a moment with my hand on my chest and took it in: Elise was "talking" to me in her sweet baby voice! She made a few more sounds and then my daughter-in-law came back on the line. "Hi, Grammie Ruth," she said, "we will be home this evening if you can call back."

As I listened to the message again, I broke down in tears.

I felt joy in the midst of chaos.

July 3, 2008 — Gordon suggested going to Dairy Queen for a chili cheese dog. It sounded like a good reason to avoid cooking dinner after a frustrating day at my office. We drove the few blocks to Dairy Queen, and he went inside to make sure they had chili cheese dogs. He came out after a few minutes signaling thumbs up, so we both went in and waited in line. I ordered a grilled chicken salad, and he ordered his hot dog dripping with hot chili and cheese. He cut it up in small pieces and ate just the meat, leaving the bun in tatters. I almost said something to him, but let it go.

Next we decided to take the car to the drive-through car wash. When the windows were covered with soap and water, I remarked on how peaceful it always is to sit in the car wash, and leaned over to give him a kiss.

"We can make out in the car in public and no one will see," I joked.

"You could take off your clothes," he said, playing along.

"No, that would be going too far," I said.

Today was a good day.

July 9, 2008 — We had an appointment with Dr. Peters, Gordon's primary care physician, to receive the results of his recent MRI and back X-rays, and also to talk about some disturbing symptoms Gordon had been experiencing. During the night, the muscles in his arms and hands would contract rather violently and his arms would fly up. If his hand happened to be on my body, the sudden grip would hurt so much that it startled me awake. Plus he had been having "shivers" or "shakes" some nights. The only thing that helped was standing up and walking around the house. We both wondered if this was another symptom of dementia, a seizure, or something else. Dr. Peters suggested we make an appointment with Gordon's neurologist.

There was always some new concern with this illness.

July 16, 2008 — We went to the neurologist to ask about the muscle jerks and shivering. She didn't think it was a seizure, but she wanted to do an EEG and a sleep study, which meant an overnight stay in a facility. Each doctor's appointment always led to one or two more. After we returned home, I made the appointments for the EEG and the sleep study. I felt concerned about how Gordon would fare during the sleep study. Would he understand what was going on and that he had to stay overnight? Would he try to take off the equipment that records his vital signs? Would he get up and wander around, feeling afraid because he had forgotten where he was? Would he tell the staff that he didn't want to stay in this strange place and ask to go home?

A couple of weeks later, I dropped Gordon off for the sleep study at about 10:00 in the evening. He seemed confused about why he was staying there, but I assured him I would come back at 6:00 in the morning to pick him up. After informing the staff that Gordon had dementia and might not understand what was going on, I drove home and fell into bed. But at 2:00 a.m., my phone rang; it was the staff from the sleep study calling to say that I must come and pick up Gordon because he was awake and wandering around. Sadly, I figured this would happen. I realized I needed to question some of the tests his doctor had ordered. They were trying their best to come up with solutions to some of Gordon's symptoms, but I was the one who lived with him twenty-four hours a day.

I began to realize that with dementia, there are never easy solutions.

July 17, 2008 — Gordon called me on my cell phone at work about 11:00 a.m. I knew immediately something was off by the sound of his voice.

"What's wrong, Gordon?" I asked.

"I just can't stop crying," he said.

"Would you like me to come home right away?" I asked.

"Yes," he said.

When I arrived, he looked distraught until I comforted him with a long hug.

Gordon said, "I am so worried that our home will be foreclosed in the next few months."

"We own our home, Gordon, and no one can foreclose on it," I assured him. "I see your Bible on the floor by your chair… have you been reading it?"

"Yes, I have. I am so worried that I'm losing my mind. I just can't handle all these worries."

We talked for awhile. "You made a good decision to read your Bible and to call me at work. Now, let's fix lunch and then you can take a long nap."

After lunch, I drove back to work and called our real estate agent, whom Gordon has always trusted. I asked him if he would talk to Gordon about our home. Immediately he replied that he would call the title company and obtain a copy of the deed to our home, put it in a folder and come by our house the next day and present it to Gordon. He said it would be an easy thing for him to do, and I thanked him. "People are so nice," I remarked as I broke down in tears. My office mate told me that I deserve for people to be nice to me.

July 18, 2008 — Our real estate agent came by with a copy of the deed to our house in a new plastic folder. He reviewed the entire document, assuring us that our house was completely paid for and that no one could ever take it away from us. The only way we could ever be in trouble is if we didn't pay our taxes, but even then it would take years for a foreclosure to happen. Gordon wanted to know what would happen if someone evil were to try to take our house. The real estate agent advised that if anyone like that came to our door we'd just say that we'd check with our agent and lawyer, and then shut the door. Gordon seemed reassured and never brought up this subject again.

Still, the insecurity bred by Alzheimer's is terrible.

July 20, 2008 — On Sunday afternoon, I was sitting on the couch reading the paper and about to doze off when I heard noises coming from the kitchen. Immediately, I went to investigate. Gordon had a tape measure and was measuring one of the kitchen cupboards. All the plates were out of the cupboard, but the upper shelf still held many heavy cookbooks.

"What's up, Gordon?" I asked.

"This kitchen cabinet is in danger of falling down. We need to go to the hardware store right away so I can buy some long screws to replace the ones that are in the cabinet," he said.

"Would you show me exactly where the problem is?" I asked.

"See these dowels here, some of them are loose," he said.

"It's okay if the dowels are a little loose. They don't hold up the cupboard, they're only there to separate the plates," I told him.

But he didn't buy that explanation and kept insisting that the cupboard could come down at any time. I continued to argue and tried to talk him out of it. Finally, I said, "Gordon, it's Sunday, and I was about to take a nap. I deal with issues six days a week, and I really need for Sunday to be quiet and free of problems."

"Well, what are you going to do when the cabinet comes crashing down?" he insisted.

Without responding right away, I thought, *"My God, what am I going to do, who can I call to ask for help with this?"* Then I thought of Bob, a man in our church who was a construction foreman for McDonald's.

"Gordon, I just remembered that Bob was a construction foreman for many years. I will call him tomorrow and ask him to come over and evaluate our kitchen cabinets. How would that be?"

Thankfully, Gordon accepted this.

I laid down to take a nap and when I felt the need of a lift later in the afternoon, I called my sister Mary, who was hosting my Mom's 90th birthday party at her independent living apartment in South Dakota. An hour on the phone with all my sisters and brothers and Mom proved to be just what I needed. Thank God for an understanding family.

July 21, 2008 — I called Bob, our construction friend, and explained the problem with the cabinets. He said he would be happy to come over and take a look, and we agreed to meet at 5:30 that day. When I arrived home from work, I told my husband that Bob would be over soon. In a few minutes, the doorbell rang and Bob and his wife Jane arrived. Gordon said, "Oh, I didn't know you guys were coming!" We invited them in and talked for a few minutes, and they complimented us on our home.

We went into the kitchen and I explained that Gordon had some concerns about the cabinets; our friend looked them over and explained they were very well built and that the dowels were decorative and didn't hold any weight. He talked about the sheer strength of the screws, and repeated himself when Gordon expressed concern that there weren't enough screws in the cabinet. Gordon still didn't seem convinced and pointed out one of the dowels that was "flapping in the breeze." Bob said that if it bothered him, we could put a little wood glue around the dowels to make them tight. We all agreed this would be a good idea, yet just before our friends left, Gordon asked if the dowels were about one-half inch down into the wood trim. Bob said he thought so.

We didn't talk about the cabinets until after dinner. "I think I'll put the plates up now that we know the cabinets are sturdy," I said. "No!" Gordon insisted. "Don't do that because I must get my drill and drill holes under each dowel and put glue in the holes."

"I don't want holes drilled across the front of the cabinet," I said.

He shrugged. "They would just be little holes," he said.

I left the kitchen in utter frustration.

July 25, 2008 — After going to bed, Gordon said, "I think I'll need a knee replacement soon." I burst out laughing. "Why are you laughing? It isn't funny!" he said.

"The matter-of-fact way you said it sounded like how one would mention they needed to replace the oil filter in the car." He laughed too.

"Have you been having a lot of pain?" I said.

"Not really," he responded.

"A person who needs a knee replacement usually is in a lot of pain and would probably be using a cane."

"It hurts a little when I get up from my chair," he said.

"You probably have a little osteoarthritis but nothing that needs a knee replacement," I assured him.

We talked about this for a while, and then he said, "We should start thinking about moving to assisted living."

I was stunned. This was the first time he had talked about that possibility.

He said, "I think it would be fun because of all the activities they have."

"We just moved to our house a year ago and I think we're still a long way from assisted living," I said.

He was telling me that he needed more to do, while expressing his concerns about aging.

AUGUST

August 4, 2008 — Our 17-year old granddaughter, Kristina, visited from Ohio for a few days. We went out for lunch and shopping at the mall with Gordon and his mother, Annabelle, who was eighty-nine and doing very well. After walking from one end of the mall to the other, we entered a big department store so my mother-in-law could do some shopping. Kristina wanted to go to a smaller store nearby, so we all agreed to meet after we finished shopping.

Before we entered the department store, we passed a small coffee kiosk, at which point Gordon mentioned that he sure would like a cup of coffee. "We already planned to go to the Cheesecake Factory for coffee and dessert after shopping," I reminded him.

We went to the third floor of the department store to the lingerie area. While my mother-in-law and I looked around, Gordon wandered around the racks of bras, panties and silky nighties. I kept an eye on him, but just as we finished our shopping, I noticed

Gordon wandering away. We paid for our items, but now Gordon was nowhere to be seen.

I tried not to panic. Immediately Annabelle and I started searching for him, and I quickly decided to inform the salespeople that I couldn't find my husband. I explained that he had dementia. They were delightfully helpful, and a couple of them started looking for him. One of the men checked the men's room, but no one was there. They paged Gordon, but I explained that he might not hear the page, much less know what to do if he did hear it. After about ten minutes, worry had overcome me and I decided mall security should be notified, as I was convinced he left the floor and was roaming a different level of the vast and busy mall. His mother, who remained by my side, was becoming tired and thirsty. She too was concerned, but seemed helpless as to what to do. When she didn't seem to realize how serious the situation was, I wondered if she had accepted that her son had dementia.

I knew that our granddaughter was waiting for us. Since I didn't have her cell phone number, I called her mother in Ohio for the number, and then called Kristina to notify her that Grandpa had wandered off and we couldn't find him. I told Kristina to come to the third floor of the department store so we would all be in the same location. Even as panic rose in me, I kept it under control. I returned to the customer service area. The women there were very helpful, and contacted mall security, at my request. By this time our granddaughter had joined us.

After a few minutes, two security guards arrived and I explained what had happened. They were calm and professional, took down a description of Gordon and assured me they would find him. They asked if I thought he would leave the mall, and I said, "It's possible."

They suggested the three of us fan out to cover more ground. My mother-in-law was fatigued, so I told her to remain in the customer service area while I proceeded to the second floor and quickly circled the area, and Kristina checked out the first floor. I passed one of the security guards, who said they were pretty sure they had Gordon in sight because he matched the description I had given them. When he said he would take me to where Gordon was, I called Kristina to tell her I was going to pick up Grandpa. We arranged for her and Annabelle to meet us at the Cheesecake Factory. Thank God for Kristina; she could take charge of her great-grandmother so I could concentrate on finding Gordon!

As I left the store with the security guard, I asked if Gordon was outside the mall, and he responded "yes." We climbed into the security van and drove all the way around the mall to the area where I'd parked the car. The guard told me the individual was standing near a car and asked me if I had parked there. "Yes," I said, knowing that we were getting closer to finding Gordon.

When we pulled into the parking lot, I saw him calmly leaning on the side of our car, drinking a cup of coffee and chatting with three security people on bicycles. The guard driving the van asked me if that was my husband, and I said, *"Yes."* I was so relieved to see him; he was not upset and didn't realize anything was wrong. When I got out of the van, I gave him a big hug. I told him I was worried because I couldn't find him. I asked him why he had come back to our car, and he responded "Well, in these situations you should return to home base." I chuckled and thanked the security guards. They had acted professionally and I was truly impressed and grateful with how quickly they located Gordon in this huge parking lot.

I decided not to question Gordon about why he left the store and what happened. By this point, I had learned these types of questions were useless to ask someone with dementia. I remarked on the rich scent of his coffee, which pleased him. In that moment I realized he had left the department store simply to buy coffee and he'd forgotten to tell me.

We hopped in the car and drove back around the mall to meet his mother and Kristina at the Cheesecake Factory. Within five minutes of going inside, we spotted his mother and our granddaughter slowly making their way toward us. We were all smiles and hugs; when I embraced his mother I whispered in her ear, "Gordon didn't even realize he was lost… he went to get his coffee."

"I knew he had coffee on his mind," she said. "I know my son pretty well!"

We all shared a laugh as we made our way into the restaurant. We didn't talk about the incident; we enjoyed our delicious cheesecake and each other's pleasant company, I have learned that staying "in the moment" is one way to cope with the chaos of dementia.

After we finished our dessert, we left the mall to take Annabelle home, but first we stopped at a drug store nearby so that Kristina could pick up an item she needed. Gordon and I and his mother waited in the car, as we were exhausted. Once Kristina returned, I backed out of the parking lot. I heard a soft bumping sound and another sound like wind from an open window or door, but when I checked, all windows were up and the doors were closed. We drove the few blocks to my mother-in-law's house, and went inside for about an hour to visit and rest. Kristina wanted a tour of her great-grandmother's house, so we did that, admired the handmade quilt on her bed, and leisurely said our goodbyes.

As soon as we stepped out of the house, I noticed that the right rear tire on the car was flat! I couldn't believe it. We all remarked on how many things had happened that day. I opened the trunk and Gordon started to take out the spare tire, but I was concerned that he would not remember how to change a tire. My mother-in-law suggested that she call her handyman, Juan, to come and help.

"No," Gordon said. "I can change a tire."

She stepped into the house to make the call anyway, when I noticed her next door neighbor, George, walking his French bulldog. I waved and he waved back, hesitating slightly as if he were sizing up the situation. He was a rather short man with a compact build, dark hair, a dusky complexion and a friendly smile. We walked toward each other extending our hands in greeting. I asked if he could help us change a flat tire. Immediately he said yes, and went right to work.

My mother-in-law came out of the house to tell us Juan was on his way over, but when she noticed we had help, she called him back and told him not to come. George was a well-to-do surgeon who was experienced with tools and assured us he had changed a lot of tires. He was matter-of-fact about it and insisted that he was happy to be of service. Kristina played with his dog, who was panting loudly in the heat of the evening. In about ten minutes, George had the tire changed, and we noticed a large screw sticking out of the flat one. The doctor mentioned how lucky we were that the tire went flat in the driveway instead of on the freeway.

George and his family were from Baghdad, Iraq. He was an excellent neighbor to my mother-in-law and I cannot help but think how ironic it is that our son Tim, Kristina's father, was currently deployed to that country with the Marines. I wondered why we were at war in their country; they were people like us who just wanted to live in peace and raise their families. I felt a need to apologize to this man for what we had done to his country, but didn't know how to begin. Instead, I reached for his hand to thank him for all his help. He pulled his hand back slightly, remarking that it was dirty from the tire, but I said it doesn't matter. We got in the car to drive home, and I felt that God had placed him in our path at the exact time we needed him.

We said goodbye again to Gordon's mother and began the slow drive home, as the spare tire was not a full-sized replacement. Gordon insisted that we stop at a service station to check the air pressure on the other tires and I started to object, but realized this was fruitless. He was trying to make sure that all the other tires were okay. We stopped and he checked the air pressure, even on the little spare. Exhausted, I prayed that God would be with us on the drive home.

As we pulled into our driveway, I reached up for the garage door opener but it wasn't on the visor where it should have been!

"I must be bad luck," Kristina said, "because this kind of thing always happens when I visit. Do you remember the time when lightning struck the utility pole and knocked out the lights and the refrigerator? I was here for that, too."

Even after we parked the car in the driveway, I still couldn't locate the garage door opener (the next day I found it wedged between the front seats), so we entered the house through the front door. We hadn't left the outside light on, so Gordon fumbled with his key for a few minutes and then rang the doorbell! Kristina tried to suppress a giggle; I remarked that I sure hope no one opens the door!

After we entered the house, I called Gordon's mother to let her know we made it home safely. I made chicken salad sandwiches for supper. After we ate, we settled down on the couch and had a good time talking with Kristina. Gordon told her about the time he got arrested for stealing gas from a car; she was very interested. We talked until almost 1:00 in the morning! It was so good to know our granddaughter in a different way that we had in the past and to see her as the lovely young woman she was becoming. Kristina told us she was writing a book, but didn't mention the topic. A few of her stories had been published in the *Marine Corps Gazette,* which has a column specifically for children of active duty Marines. She described her plans to attend college the following year and to major in psychology. We shared a group hug before heading to bed.

August 5, 2008 — At breakfast, Gordon mentioned that he'd walked a lot yesterday. I agreed and asked him what happened at the mall. He said he went to get a cup of coffee and then sat down in front of a store to wait for us. I reminded him that for quite some time we didn't know where he was, and I called mall security. He said I did the right thing; when we can't find each other, we should return to home base (in that case, our car!).

August 6, 2008 — Gordon woke me about 7:00 this morning. He was sitting on my side of the bed saying in a low voice he had something to tell me, almost like a little boy confessing a sin. I thought, "What now?" as I prepared myself. He said that at 1:30

in the morning he had woken up to find he was wetting himself. Although he'd gotten up and changed his underwear, he was still worried about the sheets and suggested they might need washing. I didn't feel any dampness, but nonetheless I stripped the bed and washed the sheets and mattress pad. I wondered how often this would happen, but I recognized his pride and dignity. I didn't want to make him feel ashamed or guilty, so I was matter of fact about the whole thing. I knew that eventually he would become incontinent.

His body had just taken another step in the wrong direction.

August 10, 2008 — We were reading the paper on Sunday afternoon when Gordon began to share something he'd seen as he was leaving church. Our pastor was holding his baby girl as he greeted the congregation. Gordon saw an older man who had recently joined our church slowly make his way over to the baby and gently put his hand on her back. Gordon broke down at this point in the story and said, "It was so touching, just to see someone move like that. I had to get out of there!"

I reflected with him, saying he had witnessed a very touching moment. Before dementia, he never would have expressed his feelings in that way. It's heartbreaking, because as the dementia progressed he began expressing his feelings in an almost child-like way. He was not so defensive; he allowed himself to be vulnerable and feel deeper than he did before he became ill. He said, "I just had to get out of there!" as if his feelings were about to overwhelm him.

Right then, I wished he had been that vulnerable and open earlier in our marriage; things could have been *much* easier.

His defensiveness, and my response to it, were major problems and often kept us emotionally distant. Until that moment, I didn't realize he was afraid of his feelings and didn't know how to express them. His emotional distance had protected him. I was always trying to pull his feelings out of him so I could receive the emotional support I needed. Now there was heartbreak and happiness at the same time—heartbreak because his illness had enabled him to become vulnerable in a way he never could before, and happiness because I had finally seen his vulnerabilities and gotten a glimpse into his soul.

Gaining wisdom can come at a price.

August 12, 2008 — This evening I talked with my mother for more than an hour, longer than I normally do. We just chatted about how our week had been, and how Dad was doing, and I shared the recent events about Gordon with her. Mom was one of my lifelines; our weekly conversations meant a great deal to me. Her deep listening and wise responses offered encouragement in the way only a mother can.

My parents were born in the early part of the twentieth century, Mom in 1918 and Dad in 1919. My dad was the youngest of nine kids; his mother died from complications of her tenth pregnancy when he was about eighteen months old. Dad always seemed lonely and emotionally aloof. He talked about wanting a mother and was envious of other kids who had mothers to call their own. If his friends complained about theirs, he would tell them how lucky they were to have a mother. One of his aunts was close to the family, and he recalled sitting on her lap, where he felt safe and loved, and wishing she were his mother.

My grandfather loved Dad and all of the other children, but nothing in his life experience had taught him how to raise nine kids alone, run the farm, and keep up with his milk delivery business as well as deal with his own grief over the loss of his wife. One way he coped was by never talking about the death of his wife or encouraging his children to talk about their mother's death. Everybody stuffed all that grief down, working hard at it, and remaining aloof and stoic. This was the way people from the upper Midwest dealt with life-altering events during the early years of the twentieth century. Mostly Dad just got "lost in the shuffle" of their household.

My mother, on the other hand, had been raised a completely different way. She too was the youngest in her family. Her sister was seven years older than she. Mom was her father's pet and little sidekick. How she loved to tag along with him while he was doing chores on the farm! She had no interest in housework and cooking. That was left to her older sister Edith. Mom had been born with a spunky personality and loved to talk. She had no experience with younger siblings and she adored being the center of attention. She also had a quick temper that flared up after she became the mother to eight children. If we wouldn't confess to who started the trouble, she would give each of us a lick with a switch, broken off from small tree branch. She said the green switches were the most effective because they wouldn't break. That didn't make the guilty party confess, but she showed us she wouldn't put up with any nonsense.

My mother and father came together with completely different personalities and life experiences. When I was a young girl, my personality tended to be more like my dad's: shy, quiet, withdrawn, and insecure. I didn't know what to say to people. Conversation could be agonizing and it was easier to take the role of the quiet observer. Now I have no problem talking to people and easily initiate conversation—people know this, as my phone is constantly ringing.

About ten minutes after my mom and I finished our conversation, I made Gordon a snack and sat down with him. The phone rang, upsetting Gordon; it was our middle son, Brian. I told Gordon to eat his snack while I talked to Brian. We chatted for about forty-five minutes, and I noticed Gordon was not eating. When I finished my conversation, I returned to fixing snacks, but almost immediately the phone rang again. That's when Gordon threw his hands up in the air and said, "I give up." I spoke with a friend for about two or three minutes. When I hung up, I asked, "Gordon, what are you upset about?"

He said, "You should know what it is."

"Do you become upset if you hear me talking to my family about you?" I said.

"I couldn't care less what you are saying; it's the time, the time. It feels like you're not here," he retorted.

I clarified this by saying, "So when I am on the phone, it seems to you like I'm not here."

"Yes," he responded.

"The phone is one of my lifelines and I don't normally talk for over two hours in one evening," I persisted. But he was having none of it.

"You talk longer than you realize!" he said.

Since he was upset and I was frustrated, I suggested we drop the conversation. We ate our snacks and soon prepared for bed. I leaned over his chair and put my head on his chest and said, "I hate it when we argue."

"Then let's not do it," he said and we agreed.

August 13, 2008 — After breakfast I felt the need to bring up the phone argument again.

"Didn't we talk enough about that yesterday?" he asked.

"We did, but I feel we didn't resolve anything," I said. "My mother and I cherish our Sunday night phone calls, and because we usually talk for only about an hour a week, I don't feel it's excessive, especially since she is ninety years old and not in good health. I wonder if each call will be our last. And I don't talk to my son very often… the two calls just happened back to back this week."

"I am not trying to keep you from talking to your family or anything like that," he said.

I knew I was trying needlessly to justify my actions, yet I couldn't let it go. When I told Gordon I knew he had never liked the phone, he said, "That is because you can never get off the thing."

We exchanged a few more words before he said, "Basically you talk too much."

I became defensive, denied the charge, and then left the room. I started crying and returned to the kitchen to tell him that my feelings were hurt.

He said, "Yeah, I shot off my mouth too soon."

After a few minutes we hugged and apologized to each other, and started over.

Later that day I read in a book on Alzheimer's that phone calls can cause agitation because the patient perceives a lack of attention. This was exactly what Gordon was saying, but I was so busy defending my right to talk on the phone, I had failed to listen to the feelings behind his words. The book suggested turning down the ringer and making or receiving calls in another room for privacy. I lowered the volume of the ringers on both handsets, resolved to move to another room to take calls, and considered changing his seat at the table so he would not be directly in front of the phone and my back would not be toward him in any way. I prayed it would help him feel less ignored.

Sometimes the simplest accommodations can make all the difference.

Fall 2008

October

October 3, 2008

I woke up this morning about 6:30, curious about what the day would be like. Gordon had not slept well because he'd moved into the guest room in the middle of the night. A little before 7:00 I heard him talking on the phone to someone. I checked the handset by the bed and it said "line busy," and I knew he had made the call because the phone hadn't rung. *Who did he call at this hour of the morning?* I wondered.

When I left the bedroom to check on him, he was walking across the living room in his underwear with the phone in his hand. He looked upset and asked me where the body was. I told him there was no body, but he said, "I saw it but now I can't find it!"

I asked him who he called and he said 911. A few seconds later he resumed his conversation with the dispatcher. Gordon gave her my youngest son Jeff's name. I picked up the extension and told the dispatcher the call was a false alarm. I explained that my husband had Alzheimer's and there was no body. I heard her relaying all this information to someone else. She asked if everything was all right and I assured her it was.

Gordon was still looking for a body, but I told him he was having a hallucination and there was no body. His eyes were wide and as he continued to pace around the room, he appeared upset and frightened. I decided to get dressed because I had a premonition the police might stop by.

Sure enough, in a few minutes the doorbell rang and a young Castroville police officer stood outside. I introduced myself and told him that the call had been a false alarm, that my husband has Alzheimer's and thought he saw a body. He expressed his sympathies; his grandmother had Alzheimer's too, he said. Gordon had put on his bathrobe and appeared at the door. The police officer asked him if he was alright.

"I guess not," he said. "It's been a rough morning."

We chatted for a few minutes and the officer left.

Gordon and I talked for a little while. He sat on the couch with his head in his hands, upset that now all of this would go on his record. I reassured him it would not go on a permanent police record; it would only be recorded at the dispatcher's office as an incoming call. He was still visibly distraught so I asked if he would like a backrub. He agreed, but first he wanted to talk more about the incident. When he again said something about Jeff, I asked if he thought the body was Jeff's, and he said yes. I assured him that Jeff was safe in Albuquerque and suggested that we call Jeff so he could talk to him. He agreed to this.

I looked at the clock. It was 7:30 our time, and I mistakenly thought it was an hour later in Albuquerque. After several rings, my daughter-in-law Sibylle answered the phone in a very sleepy voice. When I asked if I'd woken her up, she said yes. Suddenly I realized that it was 6:30 their time and apologized for calling so early. I tried to sound cheery as I said, "Well, good morning."

I explained that Gordon was worried about Jeff and asked if we could talk to him. In a few seconds, Jeff came on the line. He was on call that Saturday so he was already up getting ready for work. I told him Gordon thought he might be hurt, but I didn't mention the 911 call. I asked if he would talk to Gordon, and he said, "Sure, put him on."

I handed the phone to Gordon and he told Jeff he guessed he'd had a hallucination. I picked up the other handset and heard Jeff saying, "You're okay, what you saw wasn't real, even though it seemed real." Jeff was so gentle and understanding with Gordon, it made me want to cry. Gordon seemed calmer when they finished their conversation.

I wanted Gordon to sleep longer, but since he couldn't lie still, I asked him what he wanted for breakfast. Immediately he said, "Eggs Benedict." Fortunately I had some Hollandaise sauce mix, and in a few minutes I had poached the eggs, fixed some toast and we enjoyed our breakfast.

I was on a see-saw all the time with the unpredictability of this disease.

October 9, 2008 — I spent a lot of time locating a respite caregiver for Gordon. I found an organization called Caring Companions, and they sent us Nanette. She was quiet and soft spoken and I believed she would be a godsend. She would be coming two days a week for four hours a day. When she arrived on her first day, I suggested she take Gordon for a drive up to Medina Lake even though I knew it would cost me eighty cents per mile. It was such a beautiful October day, and I would have a couple of hours at home by myself, something I craved.

Gordon was ready to go, but it took them forty minutes to leave the house because he wanted to take coffee with him, and he was concerned about keeping track of where they were going and what the mileage was. He changed into a short-sleeved T-shirt at the last minute, and finally fixed his coffee the way he liked it. I felt anxious as my precious time alone was slipping away. I resolved that from now on, when Nanette arrived, she would be in charge of getting Gordon out the door. It was harder than I thought it would be to give up control.

About two weeks after Nanette started working, she fell at home and sprained her ankle; following that her husband became ill, so she was not able to return to care for Gordon.

Caring Companions sent two other young caregivers who would split their shifts, one in the morning and the other in the evening. This worked well until the morning caregiver took a full-time job, which she needed because she was a single mother.

After that a friend recommended a local woman who made her living as a caregiver. She cared for Gordon for a few weeks, but he did not react well to her. She talked too loudly and often spent time talking about her personal problems, which upset Gordon.

People with dementia need a calm, quiet atmosphere. I told her that she must leave her personal problems at the door and approach Gordon in a tranquil manner. Eventually I had to let her go, especially after I returned home from a grocery shopping trip and found she had not changed Gordon's briefs after he had a bowel movement.

It was a challenge to find a caregiver who was the right fit for Gordon.

2009

WINTER 2009

FEBRUARY

February 23, 2009

GORDON HAD MORE AND more trouble remembering the steps for making coffee, one of his daily rituals. Sometimes he forgot the coffee or the water, and sometimes he remembered everything but forgot to close the lid on the coffee filter basket. The pot would start brewing, but water went all over the place. Sometimes he remembered all the steps, but forgot to turn on the pot. It was extremely frustrating for him; he simply couldn't figure out what was wrong with the pot. I offered to make coffee for him, but this ritual was important to Gordon and I wanted him to continue with this activity as long as possible.

Today he came up with the solution, as he so often did. He suggested I write down a list of the steps for making coffee and *poof!* Just like that Gordon's perfect cup of coffee list was born. We posted it on the back of the cupboard door where he kept his coffee-making supplies. Most of the time, with Gordon's and God's help, I was really good at helping to execute his great ideas!

Unfortunately, it wasn't too long before Gordon couldn't understand the list or follow directions.

Summer 2009

July

July 1, 2009

I WAS BECOMING INCREASINGLY AWARE of a critical need to find adult day care for Gordon, at least one day a week. But when I'd recently mentioned this to him one evening at supper, he replied, "Thank goodness we don't need that!"

Oh, oh, that didn't go like I thought it would, I thought and started over. "I think we need to find a place for you to spend the day about once a week to give both of us a bit of a break."

He made no real response.

"I saw an ad for Mary Alice's Adult Care, which is about twelve miles from our home in Castroville," I continued. "I want to check it out."

Again, he had no response. I dropped it for the time being, not telling him that a friend and I already had an appointment to research Mary Alice's place. When we visited, my friend and I were fairly impressed. Mary Alice seemed nice, and two local doctors I'd asked about her had given me positive recommendations.

A few days later, Gordon and I visited the adult day care during lunch hour to check out the food. Gordon reacted favorably. Mary Alice explained that they were working on one of the rooms and the air conditioner. After lunch, Gordon told me he was not sure he would be able to do the maintenance work they needed. I assured him that he wouldn't be asked to do any work. He wanted to know what his purpose would be there and I explained that he would come one day a week so that both of us would have a break from each other. He could sit and read, watch television, visit with other residents, or hang out with the talking parrot. He still was uncertain and confused. I explained that I needed a day to myself, and this was a safe place for him.

Even though this seemed to satisfy him, I felt my explanation was woefully inadequate. It was clear Gordon wanted and needed a purpose for his life. I had no idea how to explain attending adult day care was his new purpose in life. I felt selfish because I knew the true purpose was for me to have a break from constant caregiving. He finally seemed to accept the idea. After lunch, we arranged for him to come every Tuesday.

July 9, 2009 — Today was Gordon's first day at Mary Alice's day care. I heard him showering at 5:30 a.m. and an hour later he was dressed and ready to go. When I remarked that he was up early, he said, "Well, I have places to go and things to do!"

I was glad that he seemed to be looking forward to going to day care. He took a short nap on the couch while I showered and after breakfast he remarked, "I'll need a hat and a pair of gloves, but I don't have any lunch."

"They will have lunch at Mary Alice's place," I said.

With that, he put on his straw hat and looked for his gloves, but came out of the bedroom with a pair of socks. He looked like he was going out to mow the lawn—it broke my heart.

We left and he put his hat on the back seat. I didn't know where he put the socks. When we arrived at Mary Alice's, he left his hat on the back seat and I asked him if he wanted it.

"No," he replied, "It's too windy to wear a hat."

We saw a kitten curled up in a little basket on the porch by the front door, and he stopped to pet it. I sat with Gordon while he had a cup of coffee and a piece of pecan pie, then gave him a kiss and hug and left. Later I had lunch with a friend, who asked me if I felt a sense of relief after dropping Gordon at day care.

"It was very hard to do because I know we have just taken one more step down a path we can't leave," I said.

July 22, 2009 — Today I learned the hard way that I simply cannot take my eyes off Gordon. As we so often did, my friend Mary Lou and I were taking a morning walk at the beautiful city park along the Medina River shaded by enormous oak trees. It was so tranquil there. On this particular morning, Gordon had joined us. We made two laps around the park, but Gordon became tired and sat down on a park bench while Mary Lou and I continued on. It was a hot, humid Texas morning, and sweat was already running down our backs. We'd only walked a short distance before I suggested we take the shortcut back to where we'd left Gordon because I felt nervous with him out of my sight. In less than ten minutes, we returned to the park bench where he had been sitting. He was gone.

I looked in the restrooms while Mary Lou slowly drove around the park. We couldn't find him, so I hopped into my car and drove around the few blocks surrounding the park. Still no sign of him. We needed help immediately. Mary Lou and I didn't have our cell phones with us, but we spotted a city public works truck. I told the driver that my husband, who has Alzheimer's, had wandered away from the park. He immediately offered his assistance and called the local police station, but there was no answer. After I gave the driver a description of Gordon, he called City Hall and asked them to alert the town meter readers to watch for him.

The public works employee drove around the park in search of Gordon. Within a few minutes the local police, alerted by City Hall, arrived. I talked to them and offered a description of Gordon. The police officers patrolled the areas around the park. Since I didn't have my cell phone with me, I drove home to pick it up and to see if Gordon had walked home. He wasn't there.

When I returned to the park, Mary Lou said she had to leave for a dentist appointment. I desperately wanted her to stay, but by then other people had heard about the situation and these earth angels were gathering around me. One lady drove all over Castroville and several people walked around the park and up the trails looking for him. By now nearly an hour passed; it was all I could do to keep myself together. If someone picked him up, he wouldn't know his address. The sheriff's deputies had joined the local police at the park. They put out an alert on the local phone system to everyone in town and even called for a rescue dog to track Gordon's scent.

A friend from church arrived and sat with me. She had called the church prayer chain and let our pastor know the situation. He also arrived within a few minutes. The police officers requested one of Gordon's shirts for the dog to sniff, so I drove home to get one. I was afraid the officers thought Gordon might be in the river, but I kept this thought out of my head, because if I dwelt on it I would have totally broken down. He had been gone almost two hours and I was worried that he would be dehydrated and exhausted.

As I gave the police officer Gordon's shirt, my cell phone rang. It was my friend Mary Lou telling me she had spotted Gordon going into the bank on her way from back from the dentist's office. She had picked him up and they were driving toward the park.

I broke down when I saw him sitting in her car, T-shirt soaked in sweat, with a big smile on his face. He didn't realize he had been lost. I told him *all* these people had been looking for him. About this time the police returned and I informed the officer Gordon had been found. He gave Gordon a bottle of water and took down my information for his records. Our pastor said that he never wanted to see my face so terror-stricken again. I went from completely stressed out to overcome with relief that Gordon was safe. We talked for a few minutes and then drove toward home. I asked Gordon why he left the park, but he had no idea. He was unaware that he had crossed a major state highway, but knew the names of some of the streets he'd walked.

I decided to take him to the new urgent care center near our house to have him checked for dehydration. The doctor examined him thoroughly and gave him more water. He was slightly dehydrated, but nothing serious and all his vital signs were normal. The doctor kept him for observation for a short while, and then we drove home. I made Gordon a sandwich after which he went to bed and slept for almost two hours.

I thanked God for the concerned people in our small town and for keeping Gordon safe.

AUGUST

August 13, 2009 — It was very clear I needed relief from the twenty-four-hour duty of caregiving for Gordon. Even though I considered this my purpose in life now, I knew I was in it for the long haul; I needed to keep myself mentally and physically healthy. I needed to accept the idea that others can take good care of Gordon, even though they don't love him like I do. He was doing very well at adult day care and after a few visits he thought he was working there. He showed me his room and called it his office. He told me he had everything he needed even though the room held only a twin bed and a recliner. I was relieved beyond words.

One night after we went to bed, he told me he needed to get some basic equipment. When I asked what type of equipment, he said he needed a printer that would print "B" size drawings because he wanted to put a detailed design package together. I was very noncommittal, and murmured, "Uh huh." He had used that type of printer in his career as a draftsman and mechanical designer; he thought he would be doing this type of work at adult day care.

It broke my heart and I started crying. I assumed he thought he would be doing maintenance work, but he was remembering his work experience! We had already turned off the lights, so he didn't notice my crying. He talked about draftsman things for a few minutes before drifting off to sleep.

I noticed his conversations were more comprehensible when we talked in bed after the lights were out. When it was dark he had no visual distractions so he could engage in a more lucid conversation. I often noticed during the daytime that if he couldn't think of a word, he substituted what he saw around him for the word he was trying to recall. He would even jump from thought to thought based on what he saw around him. The subject of work hadn't come up lately, but one time when I asked about his day, he said, "People on down the line will be waiting for me." This was consistent with his previous work, as engineers, welders and technicians would be waiting for him to finish a drawing so they could complete their work.

There was no need to tell him he was not at day care to work, but because he has dementia and can't be left alone.

FALL 2009

NOVEMBER

The day after Thanksgiving, 2009

ORDON HAD INCREASED HIS visits to adult day care to several times a week since June. This arrangement worked well for a few months, but he was declining rapidly. I wondered if he was exhausted from the emotional effort of being home for part of the week and spending the other days at day care. Even though the facility was licensed, I'd grown concerned about the care and the quality of food. One day I noticed that the owner returned from the grocery store with only some small cans of tuna, which appeared to be supper. There were no special activities provided for the residents and Gordon spent a lot of time wandering around or napping with his head down at the kitchen table.

This facility was the only one that offered around-the-clock care for dementia patients in our rural area. I dreaded making a decision to place him in full-time memory care, yet nevertheless, I had already spent time looking for a place I thought would suit his needs.

I knew the decision to move was imminent and advance preparation was critical. This choice was exhausting and heartbreaking; it was the first time I was unable to share my thinking with Gordon about a major life decision.

I decided on Homewood, a Brookdale memory care facility about a mile from his mother Annabelle's home in San Antonio and, ironically, across the street from the high school where Gordon had graduated forty-nine years earlier. Coordinating his move was extremely stressful. One day as I was driving into San Antonio from the adult day care, I blew right through a stop sign. Fortunately I was on a back country road with almost no traffic. However, this near-miss was a wake-up call that showed me I could not do it alone. *I had to ask for help moving Gordon.* I called his sons, Tim from Spicewood, Texas, and John from Tampa, Florida, and asked if they would come home to help move their father. They readily agreed.

Tim and John spent quality time with their dad while I made moving arrangements. On the day of the move, they took him to a movie while our neighbor came over with his pickup and loaded the furniture and clothes Gordon was taking with him. I timed the move so we could all have lunch together at the memory facility. Gordon's mom joined us so she could see his new home. Gordon was cooperative and liked his room and the food, but we weren't sure he truly understood he would be living there from now on.

After lunch, as Gordon took a nap, I thought it would be a good time for us to leave. Later I learned from the staff that he had been upset when he woke up and found we weren't there. I felt guilty because I hadn't taken into consideration how he would feel when he woke up, but instead was hoping to make it easier for me to leave. That evening, his mother, his sons and I went out to an unenjoyable dinner. My feelings ranged from guilt, sadness, and apprehension to relief. Guilt for leaving him in a strange place, sadness with the knowledge that I could no longer live with my husband, apprehension about how he would adjust, and relief from the burden of his full-time care.

November 24, 2009 — Today Tim and John returned to their homes and I spent the day in bed, unable to keep from crying. When I wasn't crying, I was sleeping, but would awaken again to the devastating realization that while I was living in our beautiful home, Gordon was living in half a room with a stranger who had forgotten how to speak English and reverted to his native Spanish.

November 25, 2009 — On my first visit to see Gordon today, we held hands and took a long walk around the beautiful grounds of the facility. I'll never forget his comment.

"I'm so glad we are staying in touch," he said.

"Always," I responded, "always."

December 5, 2009 — The facility where Gordon lived allowed residents, who were able, to come home for a weekend visit, which I arranged after the first few weeks. It was good to spend private time together, to snuggle and kiss and hug without other residents watching. One of the hardest things about having your spouse in a facility is the loss of your privacy as a couple. I missed "us" and our previously "easy" relationship. This was something I had not anticipated (and there are always things one doesn't anticipate!).

I tried to spend my time away from him productively. The days went by fairly well, but the evenings and nights were an agony of guilt and loneliness. I couldn't contain my grief—I didn't cry tears, but a high-pitched keen emanated from my body.

Our long-term care insurance had an allowance for bathroom remodeling, and I hired a local contactor. During the four-week construction period, I didn't bring Gordon home from the facility because the mess would be too confusing.

Before the remodeling, our bathroom had black, shiny, reflective tile flooring. As the dementia progressed, Gordon perceived it as large hole and he was afraid to step into the room. I laid towels down, but they could be a tripping hazard. The large spa tub was difficult for both of us to get in and out of, and the small, dark shower was tiled with rough-textured flooring that was uncomfortable on the feet. I had this old shower completely torn out and expanded my closet into that area. The spa tub was removed and an oversized shower was built with grab bars, a bench seat, and a large glass door, which made it easier for Gordon to shower. The floor was re-tiled with a light colored tile. The first time I brought Gordon home for a visit after the remodeling, he broke down in tears.

"It's so beautiful," he said.

2010

Spring 2010

March

March 1, 2010

Today homewood called and asked if I was coming to see Gordon, and I replied I was about to leave. When I asked what was wrong, they told me Gordon had been sitting on the floor crying because he thought I had died. *What goes through the mind of a person with dementia?* He was no longer able to logically process the reason for our living apart or to realize I would return to see him another day, so his mind jumped to the conclusion that I was dead. When I arrived at the facility he was sitting on a sofa looking sad. I gave him a big hug and a kiss and reassured him I was fine.

I was thinking more and more about hiring full-time caregivers so he could be cared for at home. But this time, I was going to be smart about it.

March 12, 2010 — On my sixty-eighth birthday, Gordon had a meltdown that precipitated my decision to bring him home. I went to dinner with a friend; our evening out was a welcome respite from my constant concern about Gordon. I arrived home around 10:00.

The phone rang and it was a staff member at Homewood letting me know Gordon had become overly agitated after dinner, so much so that he'd turned out the lights and moved the dining chairs around, threatening to throw them at staff. He grabbed a staff member by the thumb as she attempted to calm him down, pulling back on it hard, enough to dislocate it. Other staff members were unable to calm him, so an ambulance was called and he was transported to the emergency room of a local hospital. (Later I realized that Homewood should have called me right after this incident asking my permission to have him transported to the emergency room.) The staff member told me Gordon was ready for discharge from the ER and I should pick him up. He had calmed down by then, so there was no reason to admit him.

I drove to San Antonio about 11:00 that evening to pick him up from the hospital. During my birthday dinner I felt relaxed and happy, yet now my emotions ranged from worry to anxiety. But at the hospital, he was relaxed and thought he had a big adventure riding in the ambulance! The medics told me he said he just wanted to "get out of there," meaning the facility. He was apprehensive about returning to Homewood, but I had no choice. I was not ready to bring him home yet, but this incident convinced me that having him at home with full-time help was the best option for us.

During the next two weeks, I located an agency that supplied caregivers, informed Homewood I would be discharging him, and once again made arrangements with our neighbor for his move back home. This was one of the best decisions I made over the course of his illness. Not only did it mean we would live together again, but it saved me miles of driving every week and gave us both peace of mind.

Coping with Gordon's illness matured me and gave me the confidence to face unimaginable decisions. *Who can imagine making the heartbreaking decision that you and your beloved husband can't live together anymore?*

My first husband and I had lived apart for several months too. Within the first few months of our marriage, my then-husband, Denny, was recalled to active duty with the Army and stationed at Ft. Lewis, Washington. He was not allowed to bring any dependents because his unit was scheduled for deployment to Germany when the Berlin wall was built. Already pregnant with our oldest son, Steven, I quit my job at the University of South Dakota and moved home to the farm with my parents and seven younger siblings. After a few months, my husband was informed that his unit would not be shipped to Germany so he was allowed to bring his family to Ft. Lewis. I was overjoyed when Denny called saying he was coming home to pick me up.

I ran to the living room where Dad was sitting in his recliner, reading the paper. "Guess what, Dad! Denny is coming home to take me back to Washington," I announced.

"No you're not," he said.

Surprisingly, I replied "Yes, I am."

He didn't say another word. That was the only time I challenged my father. I often wondered why he had said no; I was 20 years old, married and seven months pregnant with my first child. He had no right to tell me no.

It was March of 1962 and a tremendous amount of snow covered the ground. Our old '50s-era Plymouth was buried under a huge drift. My brothers had to dig it out and plow the driveway in order for us to reach the road. Dad never liked my husband or the way he treated me; once he even said, "I can just see Denny walking out on you."

My dad's words turned out to be prophetic. Our marriage lasted seventeen and a half years and produced three beautiful sons. Before we divorced, I earned an Associate's Degree in Business Technology from San Antonio College. One day, I saw a job posting on the college bulletin board for a secretarial job at a major research and development company in San Antonio. I applied and was immediately hired. I loved this job and worked there for twenty-three years.

Occasionally I joined a group of co-workers for happy hour, which upset Denny. He was jealous of my burgeoning independence and he did walk out. Our divorce was finalized about a year and a half later.

I came into my own after the divorce, gradually gaining the confidence to express myself and my feelings. I was thirty-six years old and for the first time, I had a life of my own. I was no longer an obedient daughter and a repressed wife. I had accomplishments of my own, became fully competent at my job, and gained respect from the engineers and scientists at work.

About four years after Denny and I divorced, I met Gordon Pollard. I had overcome my shyness and insecurity and could stand up for myself. I was completely different from the quiet, obedient girl my parents had raised me to be. By now I was forty years old and ready for a serious relationship that would lead to a committed marriage. Gordon and I were married two years later.

(During Gordon's illness, I kept in touch with our five children via email.)

March 18, 2010

Hi, everyone.

As you know, I have been agonizing over my decision to put Gordon in the dementia care unit. After four months, I still was very stressed out about my decision, so early last week I gave notice to Homewood that I intended to bring him home. They were sorry to see him go; it seems he is the favorite of most all of them, but they were supportive of my decision and told me they would welcome him back if that time ever came. I picked him up about 11:00 today, and we were home in time for lunch. We are both very happy to be back together. He is fully aware that he has "checked out" of Homewood, his project there is over, and he will now be at home. When I picked him up this morning, he was sitting on a couch napping, holding a jacket (wasn't his) dressed in his red plaid shirt and brown pants, and wearing one tennis shoe and one sandal! One sock was inside out and the other was on right, but he was dressed up and ready to go! My heart melted when I saw him and I sat down beside him and gave him a big hug and kiss. My tears started flowing.

I have hired Janie, an in-home health care aide, starting on Thursday. She will be here five hours a day, five days a week to begin with, and we'll see how that goes. I haven't discussed this with Gordon yet, but this evening I will. This lady has had over thirty years of experience taking care of dementia patients, both in facilities and in people's homes. She seems quiet and soft spoken, two essentials for Gordon. I am hoping that this arrangement goes well, and will keep you all posted. Love you all, and really appreciate all the support our families have given and will continue to give both of us.

God bless all of you!
Mom

SUMMER 2010

AUGUST

August 11, 2010

GORDON FELL ASLEEP ON the couch just before bedtime. When I put my hand on his knee to wake him up, he took it and said, "Just look at that little thing." He picked it up and kissed it over and over. My tears came, and we sat like that for a while. After getting him in bed I sat next to him to give him his nightly back rub, which always calmed him and made it easier for him to sleep. He took my hand again and wouldn't let go. He was murmuring things to me that I couldn't understand. Then with a very sad look on his face he said, "I'm sorry." I told him it was alright and how much I loved him. He continued to hold my hand, close to tears. I asked him if he was sad, and he said yes. Lord knows he had enough to be sad about.

I cherished this moment.

August 12, 2010 — Gordon wears adult briefs all the time now. After having a bowel movement in his pants three times lately, today he actually used the toilet! I am filled with gratitude for the simplest things.

FALL 2010

SEPTEMBER

September 15, 2010

AT SOME POINT DURING this illness, individuals can become hypersexual. Gordon was still expressing an interest in sex, but as the disease progressed it was difficult for me. I loved him very much and wanted to express my love in this way, but it was hard for me to make the shift from changing his adult briefs to having sex. I would put him off but I always felt guilty. One night I decided to put my negative feelings aside and we had a lovely intimate experience, even though it wasn't as passionate as it once was. We lay in each other's arms afterwards, and I said, "That was so nice, it made things seem normal again."

"That's the purpose of it," he responded.

Once again in his calm, quiet way, Gordon taught me how to love.

When we attempted to make love a few weeks later, he suddenly stopped and said, "I don't like it." That was the end of our love-making.

Love-making can be the glue that holds a marriage together, even during difficult times. I missed the closeness and intimacy we always had, but dementia was robbing us of even that.

OCTOBER

October 1, 2010

Hi, everyone!

It has been some time since I have given you a more detailed update on Gordon. Things are going fairly well, and let me say that we both enjoy being together. The best decision I ever made (aside from marrying him) was to bring him home and have in-home caregivers. Whatever might happen during the day, I stop and remember how hard it was not having him here those four months, and then everything falls into perspective, because even his worst days are nowhere near as bad as having him away from home. In-home caregivers are the best way to go if you find reliable ones, and can afford it. Luckily Gordon is pretty easy to manage at home, but not all people with dementia are.

As you know, I recently spent a week in Albuquerque and Gordon stayed in the nursing home in Hondo. He came home exhausted and with a bad yeast infection from not having his adult briefs changed often enough. I will never do that again. I called them and raised holy heck, and they fell all over themselves apologizing, but that didn't help. They said they asked him every two hours if he had to go to the bathroom, but as I told them he would, he always said "no" or "eventually" or some such response. I used a nursing home for respite care as it is much cheaper that having twenty-four-hour live in care, but there are some things more important than how much money you spend, like quality of care.

Anyway, as of last week, we are now working with a full-time, live-in caregiver. The reason for this is that I can have more hours for less money paying a daily rate than if I pay the hourly rate. It doesn't mean that he has gone precipitously downhill, but rather a matter of getting the hours I feel I need for a better rate. I have been paying an hourly rate of $17.50 (quite reasonable) and the daily rate is $195. If I paid the hourly rate for 24 hours, it would be over $400, so you can see the economics of the situation. I have someone six days a week (we are by ourselves on Saturday) so that adds up to just over $5,000 a month. Our LTC insurance pays $3,800 a month for in-home care, so that leaves a shortfall of about $1,200 a month. I finally came to the realization that I will have to start taking a distribution from Gordon's annuity of $1,000 a month. I have been putting that off, but that is his money and it needs to go to his care. I am very comfortable doing that, because I want the best for him. Financially we should be okay; I have put it in God's hands so I don't worry about it. I'm thankful we have the LTC insurance and other resources.

You may wonder why I didn't do this from the start, but these decisions are made over a period of time, and it is a process that takes a while to determine the best solution. Every situation is different. Memory care units may be okay for some, but it is not for us, at least for the time being. I am young enough and capable enough to assist with his care and can make all the other arrangements necessary for help.

Gordon responds well to the caregivers. We are now using our fourth one, and he doesn't seem to mind the changes and never asks what happened to the last one. The first quit after just a few weeks due to her husband's serious illness. After that we worked with Jennifer and Angela, Jennifer in the day and Angela at night. They worked out extremely well, but when I went on vacation, the agency had to find another position for Jennifer, because she needs full -time work.

When the agency explained how in-home care would work, they sent me Juana (Janie) Avila. Not all caregivers will live in, as you might imagine. Janie is great with Gordon, but it has been an adjustment having someone here almost full time. Someone needs to be up most of the night in case Gordon gets up; they need to see that accidents don't happen and that he gets back to bed, and to change him and the sheets if necessary. I have recently discovered night-time adult briefs, and they work very well.

I have started sleeping in the guest room on my wonderful new mattress. I considered putting a twin bed in our room for the caregiver. But I found that I was not comfortable having another woman sleep in the room with him. Might sound silly, but I was not able to accept that yet. I wanted her to stay up at night and sleep during the afternoons, but she says she cannot sleep in the daytime. She tried sleeping on the couch, which I wasn't particularly comfortable with, and on at least two nights she didn't hear him get up and that caused some problems.

I realized I needed to let go of any resentment I might feel toward another woman sleeping in my husband's bedroom. Yesterday I bought a nice small recliner to go in our bedroom, and she can rest in that and will definitely hear him. I long for the days when we shared a bed, but maybe we can take afternoon naps together some time.

Janie is a very interesting person who grew up in Honduras. She has been in the U.S. for twenty-one years (legal alien status) and is working toward getting citizenship. She has had a life that none of us can even begin to imagine. Let's just say that all of us have been wealthy all our lives in comparison to how she grew up. Neither of her parents ever went to school or learned to read or write. They did not have any water or electricity in their house, and she talks of washing dishes in the river. Janie only went through third grade when her parents pulled her out of school to work, which happens with so many there. She reads and writes Spanish, and reads and speaks English quite well, but only writes a few words in English. She is forty-nine and has had six children, one of whom died as a baby. She told me that when her baby died she was so grief stricken she wanted to climb into the grave with her baby. All her children are in San Antonio with her, as well as her five grandchildren, but she divorced her husband a long time ago and there are unbelievable stories about his abuse. Considering all that has happened to her, she is very upbeat and positive and quite feisty as you can imagine. She has a strong Christian faith. I'm not sure what the story is about how she came to the U.S., but for her to have come as far as she has, basically raising her children by herself, is something I cannot even imagine. There are a few communication problems, but basically we do fine, so I am hoping this situation will continue to work. It is the nature of this business that there is quite a bit of turnover, especially as the situation changes.

As far as Gordon's condition, things do not get better. Based on my research, I am pretty sure he is in the early late stage of dementia, and this was confirmed by his doctor a couple of weeks ago. This manifests itself by his no longer being able to understand even basic directions. Most of the time he withdraws into his own world, but we can still engage him, and he responds well to other people. He is incontinent about 95 percent of the time. Even though he eats regularly, he continues to lose weight, something the doctor and I are concerned about. This is a huge problem with dementia patients. He now weighs about 147, down from his normal weight of 170. The main problem is getting him to concentrate on eating, and to keep him from becoming distracted and wandering away from the table. Our dinner plates have a red and white harlequin pattern and he was spending a lot of time tracing the pattern with his fork, so I bought some plain white plates. That made a big difference in his ability to stay focused on eating. We have three meals a day, plus three snacks, plus a supplement with Ensure or a similar product. He remembers everyone and talks about his kids and grandkids and recognizes their pictures and knows who they are. He saw his cousin Jacqui a couple of weeks ago and immediately called her by name even though he hadn't seen her for several years. He seems in a good mood most of the time and still laughs and gets off a joke once in a while. A lot of sleep is crucial; everything is much worse if he doesn't sleep enough. Some nights he will sleep ten to twelve hours, which is great, but others only five or six. We would welcome all visitors any time, but Gordon's days of travel are over. It's way too stressful on both of us. As you know, phone conversations are difficult, but I would still encourage calls because he seems to enjoy them and always knows who is calling.

Sorry for the length of this, but I feel it is important for you to know these things. I am doing great. I sleep well, go out to exercise class, walk with friends in the park, go to lunch occasionally, all in addition to shopping and of course never ending "stuff" to take care of, but I don't mind that. I go to a caregiver support group once a month and I'm now starting a dementia caregiver support group here in Castroville. Caregivers are so hungry to talk to people who are going through the same thing. I want you all to know how much I appreciate your support, and I consider it a privilege to care for Gordon. From a spiritual gifts class I took at church a few years ago, I know I have the heart of a servant, and that is fortunate, because without that it would be much harder. Please share this with your spouses and grown kids, as you think appropriate. Any and all questions or comments are always welcome.

Love you all bunches!
Mom

2011-2012

Spring 2011

April

April 14, 2011

GORDON WAS VERY TIRED this evening and would not sit down to eat. He was distracted and wandering away, so I fed him. He accepts being fed and ate a good amount. He has lost over twenty-five pounds; his body felt bony when I hugged him and his shirts hung loosely. Feeding Gordon nourishes both of us.

April 17, 2011 — Palm Sunday. Richard, our weekend caregiver, brought Gordon to church. People were so glad to see him; he did well, although he slept through much of the service. He looked through the hymnal, using his fingers to hold places in the book just as he did years ago when looking up reference material for work. He had forgotten almost everything about work yet many of the gestures he used for years are still with him.

This afternoon he needed his adult briefs changed. He was involved in sorting his sock drawer so he resisted. He came along with me but said, "It's too fucking much, it's just too much."

"Yes, Gordon," I said. "I know it's just too much."

When I looked at his ravaged body and saw the overwhelming tiredness in his face, I wondered how much longer we could bear this. His exhausted demeanor was the same as my father had several months before he died from Alzheimer's. It's a look of profound mental, physical and emotional exhaustion. I was filled with dread and deep sadness that a once vital person had been reduced to this state.

I felt heaviness in my soul.

April 21, 2011 — I woke up this morning and remembered it was the second anniversary of my mother's funeral. I miss her so much, and have many things I want to tell her. I have a good relationship with Gordon's mom, but I don't share with her like I did with my mom.

Gordon saw my picture on his dresser this morning and said, "There's Mom." When I asked him again who it was, he didn't respond so I showed him his mom's picture and asked him who that was. He said, "It's Mom."

I showed him my picture again and said "What's her name?"

He didn't reply so I said, "That's me when I was beautiful."

He said, "You're still beautiful."

I cherish these moments of closeness.

MAY

May 1, 2011 — I watched an Alzheimer's special tonight with Larry King. It was heartwarming and heartbreaking at the same time. Angie Dickenson's testimony had the most impact on me. Her sister died from Alzheimer's. She said to love your person with dementia, *not only with your heart and mind, but also with your hands and arms.* I hug Gordon many times a day, hold his hands and express a lot of physical attention. We watched the Spurs game a couple of nights ago; he sat between my legs with my arms around him for over an hour. I kissed the top of his head. Pure bliss!

At four this morning, I heard Gordon yell, "Help, help!" I went into the bedroom and Janie was up; Gordon was in bed but awake. He thought he was in the hospital and asked who all the ladies were. *Was he remembering his hernia surgery of a few months ago?*

Janie said he had been awake for about thirty minutes saying over and over, "Jesus, help me." She said he picked up a picture of me holding my six-month old grandson, Christopher, and said, "That's the one I want". His words were quite lucid. *Was he was having a moment of clarity, knowing something was wrong with him?* I sat on the side of the bed stroking his head and arms, calming him and just letting him talk.

He said, "I think about sex all the time."

"You do"? I asked. "Me too."

His vulnerability in that moment was bittersweet. Our intimacy was still intact; it was just expressed in a different way. I went back to sleep, cherishing this moment.

People ask me how I do this. God has blessed me with a compassionate and courageous heart, preparing me for this journey.

⤲

May 9, 2011 — Part of taking care of myself meant making hard choices. It was impossible to have a good night's sleep with Gordon's frequent outbursts, flailing around and getting out of bed several times a night, so I permanently moved into our guest room.

The guest room contained a double bed and matching dresser, inherited from my parents and my great aunt. I splurged on new pillows and the comfortable mattress I previously purchased. The bed was covered with my mother's handmade Texas Star quilt in bright colors of lime green, royal blue, light blue, purple, lavender and yellow on a white background. One large window looked out on the rose bushes and other plants in our front yard. A large print hung on one wall depicting a boy and a girl walking across the prairie toward home from a country school, lunch buckets in their hands. It reminded me of my childhood in South Dakota and the one-room country school I attended for eight years. My "new" room was a sanctuary; it gave me some breathing room, a quiet retreat where I could lose myself in a good book and take a nap, a respite from the daily stress of caregiving.

Moving into the guest room brought back painful memories from years earlier when we lived in our house on Ladd Road, the house we had designed and built together in the early years of our marriage. We went through a bad patch in our marriage and I was sleeping in the guest room. One weekend during that time, I saw him lying on the futon in our TV room, wearing his blue sweats, and reading a book. My heart melted; I took the book from his hands and lay down beside him.

"Hey, I'm reading," he said.

"I don't care. What are we doing, Gordon?" I asked. "We're wasting so much time being apart from each other."

He put his arms around me, and from that day on we slept in our bedroom together. Little did I know that years later I would move into the guest room again but for an entirely different reason.

Tucking Gordon in bed became a cherished part of our nightly ritual; I always told him I loved him. Sometimes he responded, sometimes he didn't. Recently he started talking about a project he was doing. "I'm just so terribly slow," he said. I tried to reassure him by telling him it was okay, there wasn't any hurry. "I'll get it done eventually," he said.

"Yes, you'll get it done eventually," I repeated. Sometimes in a lucid moment he knows he has lost the ability to plan and complete tasks he once did with ease.

I thanked God daily that he still recognized me.

SUMMER 2011

JUNE

June 14, 2011

GORDON HAS BEEN WITHDRAWN the past few days. Today he slept four or five hours, which is not unusual. He barely responded to me, even when I had jazz playing and Janie and I tried to engage him in a dance. He wouldn't sit down for supper but ate with his hands while remaining standing. Tonight when I kissed him goodnight and told him I loved him, he reached for my hand.

I know I am losing him more and more to dementia. Sometimes I'm ready for this journey to be over.

June 16, 2011 — During lunch today, Gordon was attempting to pick up an ice cube from his tea glass with his fork. He got it on the fork and started putting it to his mouth but it fell off onto his plate. A second time he attempted to pick up another ice cube with his fork and the same thing happened. I started to laugh and he smiled too. He attempted the ice trick for a third time; I decided to observe how he might solve this problem. This time he leaned over close to his fork, held the ice cube on with his thumb, but again it fell to his plate. I was in stitches by now and he was smiling too.

Finding humor on this journey saves the day!

June 20, 2011 — My prayer lately has been for just one hour with Gordon the way he was before LBD (Lewy body dementia). When things were good between us, I felt that if I died in his arms it would be wonderful. Our bodies fit together perfectly, and we were completely at ease with each other. A couple of nights ago as I was tucking him into bed, he became lucid and talkative. He told me he was worried about something and had been nervous in the Honda the other day. He talked and talked and I reassured him as best I could. He said, "I want you." Tears started to flow at that point; we talked, kissed and hugged for about thirty minutes as I sat beside him on the bed. It felt like the intimacy we shared early in our marriage.

Gordon drifted off to sleep. My prayers had been answered.

JULY

July 1, 2011 — This evening I asked our caregiver, Janie, to leave our bedroom so Gordon and I could have some privacy; I noticed she was very unsteady on her feet. Immediately I realized she was intoxicated. After Gordon fell asleep, there was a bad scene when I confronted her and she had a huge meltdown. She became defensive and started swearing. I couldn't understand most of what she said, but when she pointed her index finger at me and said something in Spanish—it felt like a curse.

I called EMS and the local police responded as well. She became very upset when she saw them and thought they were from immigration. Things went from bad to worse; she had to be tied down on the stretcher in the ambulance because she was screaming hysterically. She made such a commotion that the next-door neighbors heard it and came to see what was happening. It was absolute chaos. By the grace of God, Gordon slept through the whole ordeal.

It was hard to believe a caregiver who was so good with Gordon could be drinking on the job. I was shocked! If there had been any clues, I missed them. Janie had become a trusted part of our family, living with us twenty-four hours a day, five days a week. She was wonderful with Gordon and he always accepted her care. I prayed that she would receive help.

After the ambulance and the police left, I discovered a water bottle in the guest bathroom with alcohol in it. I called the agency that employed her and informed them of what had happened. I stressed that I no longer trusted Janie and would need another caregiver. They sent Richard for a week while finding a replacement for Janie. On Thursday, Heather came and I liked her right away, but after twenty-four hours, her back went out and Noe arrived. Thankfully Heather returned after a few days. Through it all Gordon has been rolling with the punches, accepting whoever arrived. One evening the doorbell rang and it was my friend, May, with a complete dinner.

Angels at work in our lives!

AUGUST

August 7, 2011 — I wondered how I could still love a man who poops in his adult briefs. Then he reached for me, patted my leg and said, "I love you."

That was my answer.

August 14, 2011 — The first time Gordon saw the stuffed raccoon on our church pew, he picked it up and held it all through services. After church he grabbed it by the tail and wouldn't let go. He carried it around during the pot luck lunch. I intended to return it to church the next Sunday for the stuffed animal ministry, a program contributed to by our congregants. They animals are hugged and loved on in church, and then a prayer card is attached and distributed to people who need a lift or are going through hard times.

Gordon became attached to the stuffed raccoon, so we named it Rocky. After all, he needed comforting as much as anyone else. When he saw Rocky on his bed or in a chair, his eyes lit up and he said, "Well, lookie there, he's so cute!" Sometimes he'd sit in his recliner petting Rocky and talking to him. When I tucked him at night, Rocky was in his arms.

My husband Gordon was seventy years old and had severe dementia. Rocky the stuffed raccoon was his best friend.

August 17, 2011 — I wanted to talk to our grandchildren, Anthony, age seven, and Julia, age six, about Grandpa Gordon. They were Gordon's youngest son John's children. Their mom, Jovi, is from Puerto Rico, so they have dark hair and big brown eyes. Julia's hair is a little lighter than Anthony's, and she wears it in long, soft curls. They came for a visit and when they first saw Grandpa they were looking intently at him, taking their measure of him. One morning I visited them at the bed and breakfast where they were staying with their parents. To start the conversation, I asked their mother if she had noticed anything different about Grandpa Gordon.

"Sure," she replied. "Come, Anthony and Julia, Grandma wants to talk to you about Grandpa."

"Have you noticed anything different about Grandpa Gordon?" I asked.

"No," they both said.

"Well, if you notice that Grandpa is a little different, it's because he has an illness called dementia and his brain is very tired."

"Yeah," Anthony interjected, "Daddy told me."

"Yes, I know. You might not be able to understand Grandpa when he talks to you. He can't talk good because his brain is tired," I told them.

Anthony continued drawing the picture he was working on while Julia sat in a big recliner with Shamu, the stuffed whale she had received at Sea World the day before.

"So you don't have to be afraid of Grandpa," Jovi added.

"Just remember that Grandpa Gordon loves you very much," I told them. Anthony remained quiet and serious as he continued his drawing.

"I love Grandpa forever and ever," Julia said, her arms spread wide.

Our conversation ended. I saw through their innocent acceptance of Grandpa Gordon that the single most important thing we can do for our loved ones is to love them forever and ever.

Fall 2011

November

November 2, 2011

TODAY I TOOK GORDON and his caregiver, Heather, to his mother Annabelle's house while I attended a caregiver support meeting nearby. Sometimes this works well, but I've noticed lately that he becomes very agitated when he is there, especially if the visit is too long. Sometimes I take him out for a walk until he calms down. But today when I returned to his mother's house, I could tell Gordon had had a bowel movement in his briefs.

Heather was standing with him in the kitchen looking upset. She told me Gordon had grabbed her by the arm and punched her in the chest at the same time I rang the doorbell. Sometimes sudden noises upset him. Heather and Gordon had been standing in Annabelle's office when he punched her, causing her to trip over a fan and fall. She waited while he calmed down before she took him into the small bathroom to change his briefs. She said she would call me if she needed help.

After a few minutes, I heard her call my name. When I stepped into the bathroom, I saw Heather sitting in the tub with her legs dangling over the side. Gordon had a tight grip on her wrist so she couldn't get up. She told me she was standing in front of him and when she reached around him to pull up his pants he grabbed her arm pushing her backwards into the tub causing her head to hit the wall. When I finally was able to soothe him he let go of her arm and grabbed my hand so she could get out of the tub. I led him to a chair and he slept for about forty-five minutes, after which we went home. I gave him an Ativan and he slept over an hour.

I have always hoped that Gordon wouldn't become violent, but if this continued I won't be able to keep him at home. He has never been aggressive with me or a male caregiver. Heather suffered a mild concussion as a result of her fall into the bathtub. She did not return to care for Gordon. There is always some new horror to face with this damned disease.

He had what is called a catastrophic reaction, which can be caused by a mistake made by the caregiver. I think what set him off was his caregiver's position in the bathroom. She was standing in front of him as she reached around him to pull up his pants, violating his physical space. He may have felt it was an unwelcome hug. If she had stood behind him to pull up his pants, he might not have had a violent reaction. As this disease progresses, the person's ability to think logically is greatly diminished. Not all catastrophic reactions are caused by a caregiver's mistake. Sometimes the frustration and confusion of the damaged brain will cause a person to lash out.

November 5, 2011 — I told Gordon's caregiver, Richard, that my youngest son's forty-first birthday was November 6th. He remarked that he wished he was forty-one again. I said, "Not me, but maybe so, because I was forty-one when I met Gordon."

Gordon was listening and said, "It's been hell ever since then."

I replied that I thought every day had been pure bliss. We all had a good laugh!

After breakfast Richard was coaxing Gordon to take his meds and saying, "Here Gordon, take your meds." He repeated his request about three more times; Gordon mocked him by imitating the way he said it. Then Gordon said, "Cut that shit out." We had two good laughs in one morning.

November 25, 2011 — I showed Gordon a picture of me holding our eighteen-month-old granddaughter, Elise. He looked at it and said, "Oh, lookie here." Then he took the picture and cradled it in his hands, saying something muddled. I understood only two words, "wish" and "alive." He pointed to my face with his thumb. I said, "That's me," to which he responded, "I know." Didn't he realize that the person in the picture was alive beside him? Another mystery I'll never solve.

As I typed these notes a few years later, I believe Gordon was saying he wished his daughter Tammy were still alive. The little girl on my lap may have reminded him of Tammy, who took her own life at age forty-five in 2007. Her death was very upsetting to him at the time, but I always felt the immensity of it never really hit him. Perhaps one blessing of dementia is that it protects him from remembering the traumas in his life.

Tammy was Gordon's oldest child and only daughter. She was born on May 3, 1962, and she was declared dead on June 2, 2007, a month after her forty-fifth birthday. Her body was found that day, but no one knows the exact date and time of her death. One day towards the end of May, she climbed into her bathtub, tucked a gun under her chin, and pulled the trigger. What a violent, horrible way to die, alone in her apartment.

She had Dancie, a little female Chihuahua she found several years earlier near her apartment building, abandoned in a cardboard box, but with a small dish of water beside her. Before she took her life, she shut Dancie up in another room and left a dish of food and water for her. Tammy was a loving and caring person, but tragically she didn't love herself enough to continue living. We will never know what drove her to this act of despair and violent self-destruction. Trouble seemed to follow Tammy like a dark, threatening storm cloud.

In order to better understand suicide, I read Edwin S. Schneidman's book, *The Suicidal Mind,* in which he states:

> "Psychological pain is the basic ingredient of suicide. Suicide is never born out of exaltation or joy; it is a child of negative emotions."

I asked myself what signs did her dad and I miss; what did her brothers and mother and stepfather miss? Could we have intervened, and helped her to understand how much she was loved? Would she have believed us? But she chose the path of suicide, the path of self-destruction, the path of darkness, and the path of hopelessness that day in May when she climbed into the bath tub and pulled the trigger, ending her pain forever.

WINTER 2011 – 2012

DECEMBER

December 1, 2011

Today I placed Gordon in Horizon Bay, a memory care facility in San Antonio, Texas. After the incident with Heather, finding a good caregiver had become increasingly difficult. Gordon's doctor strongly recommended that I place him in memory care. I had been searching for a place where I felt comfortable in anticipation of this need. The caregiving staff there was wonderful and very attentive toward their residents. I liked the way the facility was designed with shorter, wide hallways placed around a central living and eating area. This area had lots of comfortable easy chairs and a couple of long dining room tables with chairs placed around them, giving the space a homey feeling. The kitchen was readily accessible and visible but I noticed the refrigerator doors were locked. Gordon soon became one of their favorite patients.

To make the transition a bit easier before we moved him, I said, "Tomorrow you're going to another project."

"I appreciate you telling me," he responded.

I wanted to hold him tight and say, *"No, no, that's not right; you are going to stay home with me."* I felt like I was betraying him and lying to him. But I have to remember, we lie to the disease, not to our loved one.

Once again my friends and neighbors willingly pitched in to help move his furniture. Fortunately, he had a private room which would make our visits so much easier.

I realized this placement would be his last, and I knew this was the best option for us. But still, it was heartbreaking because Gordon was not able to help make this decision. I made it for him, and because of that I felt a twinge of guilt rubbing against my heart. However, on moving day, he seemed happy and settled in easily. Rocky the Raccoon went with him.

December 15, 2011 — Today Gordon was upset and pacing around his room. "I'm worried," he said.

"You are?" I responded.

"Well, of course," he told me.

I didn't pursue the conversation and let it drop. Years later it still haunts me. Why did I let the conversation fade away? Was I afraid of his response? Was I unsure what my response would have been? Because he had severe dementia, did I think he wouldn't be able to tell me? If I had questioned him, I might have comforted him and set his mind at ease. I tried not to second-guess my decisions, but I missed an opportunity for him to share his fears.

A few days later, Gordon's son Tim came to visit. Of his three children, Tim looks the most like his dad and their mannerisms are similar. In fact, when I first met Gordon, he had an attractive beard; we had been married only a few months when Gordon went to town to get his hair cut. When he came home, not only did he have a haircut, but he had asked the barber for a professional shave. I was stunned! He hadn't told me ahead of time that he was going to have his beard shaved off. He looked so much like Tim it startled me for a minute... that is how close the apple fell from the tree.

Gordon had a good sense of humor and enjoyed an off-color joke, even in the late stages of dementia. Tim was in fine form on the day of his visit; he would crack a joke and Gordon would let out a good laugh. The more he laughed, the more jokes Tim would tell. This went on for a good thirty minutes. When it came time for Tim to leave, he gave his dad a big hug.

"Goodbye, John," Gordon said as Tim left the room. As I walked Tim out of the building he said, "Dad doesn't know who I am. He called me John."

"He knows you are his son," I reassured him. "He just misspoke when he called you John."

I think it's particularly difficult for children to accept a parent's dementia. They have known their parent for their entire life, and adjusting to the new reality is an enormous feat.

JANUARY

January 1, 2012 — I drove to Horizon Bay to wish Gordon a Happy New Year. As I looked around the dining room for him, I saw an old man sitting at the table. I thought they had a new resident.

The man was wearing a gray T-shirt that said "Army" in big, black letters. I was stunned to realize it was Gordon. He was sitting at a dining room table, his head thrown back, eyes shut and mouth gaping open. The caregivers told me he had been like that all morning. When they tried to get him out of the dining room chair, he could no longer stand or walk so they placed him in a wheelchair and took him to his room and helped him to his brown recliner. Now I knew the year of his death would be 2012. Three days later he was under hospice care.

The hospice staff was wonderful, kind and caring. They provided everything Gordon needed, including a hospital bed with an inflatable mattress to help prevent bed sores. He wore inflatable "leg warmers" to help prevent blood clots. They provided his adult briefs and all toilet articles. His doctor took him off all his meds. Since he slept in the hospital bed, his twin bed was available for me to rest on. I moved his brown recliner right next to his bed so I was close enough to hold his hand, which he accepted quietly, while I read to pass the hours. His TV was across the room, but I rarely turned it on. Because of his illness he was no longer able to concentrate on it and I didn't want the distraction. The room was at the end of the hall; it was large and quite comfortable with ample room for the caregivers.

January 15, 2012 — I talked about death so calmly and said the word easily, but I didn't know anything about it. I was learning. Learning about it at 11:00 a.m. on the day I spent about two hours with him, gently trying to feed him and coax him to suck water from a straw. The most basic, elemental thing etched in our genes is the knowledge of how to suck, even before we are born. Now he had almost forgotten even that. How long can a body live that can't suck fluids anymore?

Alone in bed that night, the panic and grief rose up in my chest so I could hardly breathe. Sobbing tears came; I grabbed my journal and pen, hoping to keep the grief at bay a little longer, trying to distance myself a bit. I was beginning to feel the reality of Gordon's death; he really was going to die soon. I'd never again be able to hold his hand, hear his voice or see his warm brown eyes. His eyes were closed most of the time now; that was the hardest thing, not being able to look into his eyes. This afternoon, I cranked up the head of his bed to make it easier to feed him; the movement of the bed startled him and he opened his eyes for a few seconds. I said, "Great, Gordon, you opened your eyes!"

He looked at me; I couldn't quite tell if there was recognition there, but he said, very weakly "great." His lips curved into a small smile.

"Great." It was the last word he said to me.

January 17, 2012—During the last few days of his life I visited him almost daily. I spent long hours sitting in the recliner beside his bed, holding his hand and reading *Half Broke Horses* by Jeannette Walls. He ate and drank very little, some days almost nothing. The caregivers and I dipped a straw in liquid and brushed it lightly over his lips. Sometimes this elicited a sucking or licking response, but mostly it didn't. He was completely bedridden, but the hospice aids showered him every few days. They were doing such a good job of keeping him clean. They put a clean T-shirt on him every day.

I wondered what the lumps were under his sheet. When I lifted it, I saw his rib cage and his hip bones. He had lost so much weight! How much longer can a body live? I sat on the edge of the bed caressing his head and arms and telling him over and over that I loved him. The caregivers swabbed his dry mouth with small sponges on a stick, like a lollipop. Sometimes he bit down on them and they had to work to pull it out of his mouth. I wondered if he thought it was something to eat. Or possibly it was an automatic response to feeling something in his mouth.

Six days before he died he stopped eating. If we put a tiny bite in his mouth, he "pocketed" it in his cheek; the nurses told me the body can live seven to ten days without food and water. I wondered how he could possibly live that long. He was basically living off his body. It was heartbreaking seeing him like this; at times I couldn't hold back my tears. Yet I knew he could still hear, and I didn't want him to hear me crying.

January 21, 2012 — At 11:00 p.m. Saturday, the hospice nurse called me at home to ask for my permission to give Gordon a dose of morphine. She told me they put him on oxygen because he was working so hard to breathe. I gave permission for the morphine; she said it would relax him. I awoke his son John who had been with me since the 18th; I told him I wanted to leave early in the morning to see his dad.

❦

January 22, 2012 — John and I arrived at Horizon Bay at 7:30 Sunday morning. I had packed a bag, for I would not leave Gordon until he died. As he lay in the hospital bed next to the window, I washed his body. I wanted him to feel my hands on him, to sense my presence in his last hours. I wanted to do something physical that would allow me to release him. I was stunned by his weight loss—he was just bones. His body was limp; he showed no reaction to being touched. The bath was the last thing I did for him.

I spent the last day and a half sitting in his brown recliner next to the bed holding his hand and finishing *Half Broke Horses*. The twin bed where I slept the last night of his life was across the room next to the bathroom, covered with a light-blue bedspread. A small TV sat next to the closet where a few of his clothes hung, clothes he no longer needed. An oxygen concentrator wheezed noisily next to the recliner. The hospice nurse sat in another chair in the corner ready to assist him.

About 11:00 o'clock Sunday evening, the hospice nurse informed me that Gordon was close to death. The oxygen was still on and he was breathing easily. They gave him a tiny morphine pill, which quickly dissolved under his tongue. I prepared for bed wondering if I would sleep. The oxygen concentrator was noisy and the hospice nurse was in the room, but I fell asleep right away.

❦

Monday, January 23, 2012 — I woke up once during the night and heard the concentrator so I went back to sleep. When I awoke at

5:00 a.m., I couldn't believe I'd slept all night. Gordon's breathing sounded different; the hospice nurse told me the change in breathing signals the end is near. I called John and asked him to come immediately; he arrived less than an hour later. I called Pastor Lynne who arrived about 7:00 a.m.

John was such a rock for me. He had his iPad with him and selected some of Gordon's favorite songs, Tom T. Hall and Patsy Cline. Gordon gave no indication that he heard the music or sensed us near him. His face remained impassive and composed, his body completely relaxed. The hospice nurse informed us what to expect in this stage when he was actively dying. She said the sense of hearing was the last to go. I knew it was time to let him go; his breathing was growing slower and slower. We decided to remove the oxygen tube; the nurse said it was not helping. It was quiet in the room without the huffing sound of the concentrator. John, Pastor Lynn and I were at his bedside. Pastor Lynn prayed for several minutes. His breaths were shallower and further apart. "I love you, Gordon," I said, and he took one more small breath. I was calm and felt no panic, just a deep sense of peace. I was with him in his last hours, loving him and honoring our love till death parted us.

We spent some time at Gordon's bedside alone until several staff members arrived to offer their condolences. Many of them were crying softly; they had become so attached to Gordon in the two months he was a resident. John and I were hesitant to leave, but we knew we had to tell Gordon's mother of his death. The hospice nurse assured us that she would remain with his body until we returned.

John and I drove to his Grandmother Annabelle's house. Pastor Lynn followed in her car. She graciously offered to go with us and I was so thankful for that. I didn't know how Gordon's mother would react; she knew her son was dying for several days, but still I expected a very emotional scene. I needed help dealing with her emotions. I couldn't fall apart now because there was still a lot to handle when I returned home. As soon as Annabelle opened her door and saw us outside, she realized why we were there and broke down in tears.

"Oh, no, my boy, my boy is gone," she said over and over.

John and I comforted her as best we could; Pastor Lynn offered a prayer, which helped calm Annabelle. She got dressed to see her son's body for the last time.

When we entered Gordon's room again, I noticed the hospice nurse had placed a rolled-up, pink-and-blue striped bath towel under his chin. He would hate that pink and blue towel under his chin; I knew it was there to keep his mouth from gaping open. I just wished they had used his brown towel. Annabelle was fairly composed when she saw Gordon's body, but we all shed some tears. I knew it was hard to lose your husband, but I couldn't imagine how much harder it would be to lose your son. She tenderly stroked his head over and over. She said she was so glad she got to see Gordon's body; it helped her to accept his death.

We spent about thirty minutes at Gordon's bedside before it was time to leave. I asked the hospice nurse if she would stay with his body until the crematorium arrived. I worried about him being cold and asked her to leave his T-shirt on. After we drove Annabelle back home John and I returned to my house and started making endless arrangements. Later on I wondered if I should have accompanied

Gordon's body to the crematorium. I asked myself, *how did I walk out of his room leaving him there?*

At home, I called Gordon's oldest son, Tim, to let him know of his father's death. Then I called his oldest sister, Linda, and asked if she could call her two younger sisters. I called my sister, Maggie and asked if she would please call our six younger siblings. I couldn't face making all those calls, relaying Gordon's death over and over again.

John started putting together a memorial service for the coming Saturday morning at 11:00 o'clock at the Medina Valley United Methodist Church in Castroville, Texas. I hadn't written his obituary ahead of time, so I started writing it to meet our local newspaper's deadline.

Over the next few days, I attended to a myriad of details, making calls and receiving many condolence calls. Gordon's oldest son, Tim, and his wife, Sharon, arrived from Spicewood, Texas, and Pastor Lynn came to the house to plan the memorial service. I wanted some input from his sons but I would make the final decisions. Tim and Sharon were upset when I didn't take their suggestion to sing "Amazing Grace." It is a beautiful song, but I felt it was overused at memorial services. Fortunately, Pastor Lynn kept us all on an even keel.

My three sons, Steven, Brian and Jeff all lived in Albuquerque, New Mexico, so they were not with me for the planning; but they all arrived for his memorial service. It was a great comfort having our five sons with me.

John literally spent hours putting together a slide show depicting Gordon's life; it would be shown at the memorial service and luncheon to follow. It turned out beautifully. The funeral committee called to make arrangements for the luncheon. I estimated about 150 would attend, filling the church.

෬

January 25, 2012 — It was a lovely Texas winter day, warm and sunny. I wore black slacks, a white blouse and a black and white tweed jacket. Our immediate family gathered in the fellowship hall, waiting for guests to arrive. Annabelle, two of his three sisters, all five of our children and two daughters-in-law, one of my brothers and his wife, and two grandchildren attended, giving me the support and love I needed. When it was time for the service, I walked into the church hand in hand with Annabelle, followed by our families. The church was full and I was amazed to see many people I had not seen for a long time. There were many friends from church as well as people who worked with Gordon and me. We took our seats in the two front pews and the service began. I noticed several beautiful bouquets of flowers on the altar, including an extra-large one given by our former employer, and the 18" x 20" portrait of Gordon. But he wasn't there.

The service went smoothly. His son John spoke and was interrupted once when his seven-year-old son Anthony started talking. The congregation sang one of Gordon's favorite songs, "Washed in the Blood of Jesus." We closed the service listening to a recording of The Lord's Prayer sung by Andrea Bocelli. It was beautiful and moving. I kept my composure; I wanted to enjoy every second.

There would be time for tears in the days and weeks to come.

FEBRUARY

February 17, 2012 — Last night I dreamt about Gordon for the first time since his death. I was in a large office building looking for him. He was in a meeting, but I wasn't sure exactly what room he was in. I heard a group of people come out of an office, talking and laughing. I wondered if Gordon was with them; then I heard his laugh. It sounded so real. I saw him and said, "Here I am, Gordon, are you ready to go?"

He came to me, lifting up his shirt. He was moving along very rapidly, almost floating. I called out to him telling him he should stay with me so we wouldn't be separated. There were lots of people around and I was afraid I wouldn't be able to find him, but he kept on going into another large room. Suddenly he came out the other side, riding something like a four-wheeler. He seemed energized, happy and free. When we came to several flights of stairs, he took off on his four-wheeler riding down the stairs, again almost floating. I thought he would fall, but he didn't. I saw him go down three flights of stairs very smoothly.

Then he was gone, my dream over.

MARCH

March 1, 2012 — This evening Charlie Rose interviewed William Shatner about the death of his loved one. William Shatner openly said that his loved one's body looked small, and he wondered how it had happened—how did this vital, lively person suddenly become so small in death? Gordon had lost a lot of weight; in death he looked even smaller. When his mother saw his body, she said, "He looks so small." Maybe it's our spirit, our soul that makes us look larger in life; and once it leaves, the body deflates, becomes smaller. During the conversation between Charlie Rose and William Shatner, my tears started flowing. Gordon's death was again fresh in my mind.

March 31, 2012 — Today was our twenty-eighth wedding anniversary, an incredibly difficult day, even harder than the day Gordon died. Our wedding seemed so long ago but I remembered it clearly. As I looked at our wedding pictures and saw how young our children were (and how young we were!) I wondered, "Where did the years go?"

Over the past few days I went through Gordon's clothes. I threw out anything that was stained or worn and washed all the rest, folded them neatly, and stacked them on our bed. His best pair of shoes was there too. I kept his favorite blue, tropical-print shirt and wore it for a while as I worked. The next day I put the clothes in garbage bags and took them to a local church clothing ministry. I cried, seeing his unworn clothes, his empty shoes.

His closet, empty except for a few hangers looking like skeletons, the black box containing his ashes, the large 18" x 20" photo of him smiling beautifully, wearing his blue shirt, seemed a shrine to him, a place for me to shed my grief tears.

2014-2016

Winter 2014

January

January 23, 2014

It was a "tender day," two years since Gordon's death. He was on my mind this morning. I talked to him and told him I loved and remembered him. I told him our marriage was wonderful, not every day, but taken as a whole it was a wonderful twenty-eight years. It had passed in the blink of an eye.

Grief has stayed with me, not the dull ache, frustration and despair I sometimes felt during the years I cared for Gordon or the sharp pain the day he died. When I became vulnerable enough to love Gordon for better or worse, I opened myself to joy as well as grief. Now grief is softer, tinged with beautiful memories.

Sometimes grief visits in unexpected moments. Seeing an older couple walking hand in hand, watching sailboats on a lake, hearing a Patsy Cline ballad, or experiencing the easy sway of a jazz recording all remind me that I will never share those times with Gordon again. To feel grief over Gordon's loss is a reminder that we loved each other for twenty-eight years.

We wanted more time together, but now I cherish the time we had. Grief is okay. It tells me I shared a portion of my life with a wonderful man. I would rather feel grief over his loss than feel regret that I hadn't taken a chance on love.

Summer 2016

The Final Goodbye

June 29, 2016

O N A HOT, SUNNY afternoon on beautiful Travis Lake, Texas, the Pollard family gathered to say our final goodbye to Gordon David Pollard: son, husband, father, father-in-law, grandfather, and great-grandfather. Four and a half years had passed since his death on January 23, 2012. Gordon and I had talked about what to do with our ashes. After the death of his daughter Tammy, we decided we wanted our ashes intact, not scattered, which was her wish. We didn't have a burial plot. Gordon loved the water and it seemed the best place to put his ashes. I spent a lot of time thinking about how to accomplish this. I chose Travis Lake because it was about a mile from Tim and Sharon's home, his oldest son and daughter-in-law. The date was chosen because his youngest son, John, his wife, Jovi, and their two children, Anthony and Julia, were on a cross-country camping trip and would be in Texas. It would be easy for his grandson Matthew and his family to travel from Killeen, Texas. His granddaughter, Kristina, also lived in the area.

I flew from Albuquerque, New Mexico, to San Antonio, Texas, carrying Gordon's ashes in the biodegradable urn I had purchased. I was apprehensive about going through security with the urn, but the people there were very respectful when I informed them I carried human remains in my small carry-on bag. After landing in San Antonio, I drove to Boerne, Texas, where Gordon's ninety-seven year old mother, Annabelle, lived in a private care home. I stayed in a bed and breakfast close to her home. I was exhausted when I arrived and slept nine hours that night. I picked Annabelle up on the morning of the 29th and we drove to Travis Lake. Sharon had rented a party boat from the marina large enough to accommodate our group of fourteen. Annabelle needed a wheelchair outside of her home. She was uncertain about boarding the boat, but decided if she didn't do it, she would regret it. We wheeled her onto the boat and the chair fit perfectly. A large umbrella had been provided to protect her from the hot Texas sun. With John at the wheel, we took off to find a good spot to toss the blue, biodegradable urn.

Travis Lake was beautiful and completely full thanks to abundant spring Texas rains. We found a place we liked and dropped anchor. To break the ice and start the memories flowing, I talked about the first time I saw Gordon walking past my desk and thought, "Who was *that*"! He was so good looking. Then others began sharing their memories: how grandpa taught grandson Matthew to fish; how he taught son Tim a tongue twister to help him learn to pronounce the diphthong *st*; how he loved beer and country music, specifically Tom T. Hall; about some of the trouble he got into when he was a teenager, like the true story of the time he placed a trash can full of water on the train tracks and watching the train smash into it (he got caught), and his love of motorcycling and sailing.

Once everyone had a chance to hold the urn and share their memories, his son Tim took the urn and threw it off the back of the boat. It made a big splash! We all sat for quite some time watching the lovely blue urn bobbing up and down in the water. The sun sparkled on the lake like floating diamonds. The wake from a passing boat pushed the urn towards a sheer, rocky cliff, covered with ivy. As we pulled away, the urn was beginning to sink.

After we returned to the marina we regrouped and enjoyed a delicious lunch at It's All Good Bar-B-Q, and ordered some of Gordon's favorite foods. We celebrated three family birthdays: granddaughter Julia, eleven on June 29th, great-grandson David, two on July 1st, and mother Annabelle, ninety-seven on July 5th. The restaurant provided slices of pecan pie with a candle for the birthday people.

In this instant, my heart felt full with gratitude for the gift of true love with a man whom I was able to love and care for during our marriage and especially during the last six and a half years of his life. Gratitude for the heart of a caregiver, a gift bestowed by God, overwhelmed me, along with thankfulness for the gift of family, one that held me together as I let Gordon go.

Goodbye, my love.

Epilogue

B Y THE TIME GORDON was diagnosed with dementia, I had matured, developing the skills I needed as his primary caregiver. The organizational and multitasking skills I learned from my mother, during business school, and at my secretarial job all allowed me to organize a care team for Gordon and to accomplish many daily tasks by effectively directing the work of the live-in caregivers. I learned to speak up for myself and to ask for help, both useful caregiver skills. I asked neighbors and friends to stay with Gordon when I went shopping, ran errands or enjoyed an occasional lunch with friends.

I also accompanied him to his doctor's appointments, asking questions Gordon could no longer ask. Researching medications online and finding websites gave me information about dementia in general and, specifically Lewy body dementia. My love of reading, fostered by my mother, aided me as I read many books on all aspects of caring for someone with dementia. My love of education inspired me to attend classes on how to be a caregiver; I kept my eyes and ears open learning as much as I could about this awful, brain-robbing disease.

I took care of Gordon until his death, six and a half years after his diagnosis. As the illness progressed, he became more childlike and dependent on me. We drew closer to each other because we knew our time together was limited. Gradually his defensiveness gave way to openness and acceptance. Gradually my impatience and frustration gave way to patience and tolerance. Taking care of my husband was so much more than mere duty; I loved him, doing my best to make the most of each day, each hour. I "went into his world" accepting him as he was. Through education, help, and support, I made our journey through dementia as loving as possible.

I have experienced great change and personal growth since Gordon's death. Six months later, I sold our Castroville, Texas, home and moved to Albuquerque, New Mexico, to live near my three sons. My oldest son, Steven, is a tall, white-haired chef and his girlfriend, Siobhan, gardens and takes care of Steven and their dog, Vasser, and cat, Charlie. She also works as an extra in New Mexico's film industry. They like to take road trips around New Mexico and adjoining states. My middle son, Brian, is a clinical psychologist with the New Mexico Army National Guard, and his wife, Misty, is a social worker who works with emotionally disturbed children at a local hospital. Both Brian and Misty have completed marathons in almost all fifty states. Their three children are Ericka, thirty-two, a technician with a local computer company, Renae, twenty-nine, and Jon, twenty-six who share an apartment and work in Utah. My youngest son, Jeff, is a prosthetist/orthotist, and his German-born wife, Sibylle, is a diagnostic sonographer. Their children are Christopher, a tall thirteen-year-old eighth grader who loves Junior ROTC, and Elise, a blond eleven-year-old sixth grader who loves dancing and walking their dog, Thor. Knowing my grandchildren has been wonderful; they have given me a new focus on life.

Gordon's oldest son, Tim, is retired from the Marine Corps and he and his wife Sharon live in Spicewood, Texas. Gordon's youngest son, John, is retired from the Army National Guard, and he and his wife, Jovi, and their children live in Valrico, Florida.

Now at age seventy-five, I hope I have been a role model to my precious children and grandchildren. I believe I have given them the strength of character my parents gave me, and have shown them how to cope with adversity. It is possible for a single, active, involved woman to have a happy productive life even after the death of a beloved spouse.

A friend whose husband recently died said, "I have stopped looking back at what I lost and am looking forward to what is next." My work as a facilitator for caregiver support groups for the Alzheimer's Association gives me a new passion and purpose.

I, too, have stopped looking back at what I lost and look forward to what is next.

ABOUT
GORDON DAVID POLLARD

G ORDON DAVID POLLARD WAS born to Annabelle and Claude Pollard on April 7, 1941, in Ft. Dodge, Iowa. Gordon was fifteen months old when his father died unexpectedly from a blood clot following an appendectomy. This tragedy had life-long consequences for him, but also shaped the man he was to become. After her husband's death, Annabelle moved from their farm house and into a small apartment in Boone, Iowa, with her mother, who took care of Gordon when Annabelle went to work in the Wards catalogue ordering department, and then for a company that packaged soap, where she became the supervisor of the shipping department. She purchased a small home on Crawford Street in Boone. She also went back to school to study clothing design and construction. She has said her strong faith in God helped get her through this terrible time.

His mother, Annabelle, is still living at the time of this writing. She is ninety-nine, and recently I asked her what Gordon was like as a child and young person. "He was always so nice, he was just so nice," she said.

When I asked if he was mischievous, she said, "of course" and shared a recollection. "Once he threw one of his toys in the toilet. The plumber was called and our landlady was very unhappy. I give my own mom a lot of credit for the way Gordon turned out. After Claude died, I was in shock and didn't know what to do. She helped me raise him."

She continued, "I don't remember a lot from that time, but I always knew where Gordon was. He usually ran down the street to play with the neighbor kids. His Pollard grandparents made a big fuss over him, as he was their first grandchild and Claude's son."

When Gordon was six or seven, his mother married his stepfather, Carl Abbenseth, and the family moved to San Antonio, Texas, where Carl was an airplane mechanic first with Slick Airways and later with Eastern Airlines. Annabelle gave birth to Gordon's three sisters, Linda, Bonnie and Deborah. Gordon missed small-town life with his grandparents nearby, and once when his mother came home from a meeting at her church, she found him sitting in the car. "I want to go back to Boone!" he said. As he got older, he spent summers in Boone with his Pollard grandparents and cousins.

There was trouble with his stepfather, including some physical and mental abuse. Gordon told me that when he was about thirteen years old he fought back, which stopped the physical abuse. About the time Gordon turned sixteen, he moved to Chicago to live with his father's brother, Bob. He completed his junior year there, but moved back to San Antonio for his senior year, graduating from Robert E. Lee High School in 1960.

Gordon was a good student, but also liked to have fun, date girls and ride his motorcycle. He loved to ride to the Texas Hill Country camping out by himself. And he was still mischievous. He recounted the tale of when he and a friend placed a large aluminum garbage can full of water on the train tracks that ran close to their house. They watched to see the water-filled trash can explode. But someone had seen him and identified him to the railroad authorities. Later the police knocked on their door. It probably wasn't one of Gordon's best days! Another time he and a friend syphoned gas from a car, but the police saw him. (This is the story our granddaughter, Kristina, loved hearing him tell the night the three of us bonded, shortly after he developed dementia.) Busted again! I think this put an end to his criminal career.

People tell me Gordon was so easygoing, and that was one trait that attracted me. He worked hard, but knew how to relax. He owned a catamaran for a few years and loved sailing on the Texas coast. Once he crewed a sailboat on a trip across the Gulf of Mexico from Houston to New Orleans. He was always ready for a good laugh and loved sharing beers with friends or his sons. His dry sense of humor and wit always lingered just under the surface.

After high school graduation, Gordon enrolled at the University of Houston. He took courses in drafting and mechanical design, and found he had an aptitude for this type of work, which set him on his career path. He did not return for his sophomore year at the university, but instead found a job with a company that was hiring drafters. Much of his knowledge in his chosen career was learned on the job. About this time, Gordon met his first wife, Sonja Gay Sparks. They married in 1961 and Tammy was born in 1962, Tim in 1964 and John in 1966. They continued living and raising their family in the Houston area, but the marriage only lasted about seven years. Gordon has said, "We were just too young when we got married." Jobs were plentiful in his field and he worked in several towns in South Texas, New Orleans, and for a brief period on an oil rig in the Gulf of Mexico. He and a friend and co-worker established their own drafting and design company for a few years. His children remained in the Houston area with their mother and step-father, but spent school holidays and summers with Gordon and his second wife Carol. His kids remember there was a big pot of beans on the stove and "campfire glop," which was basically scrambled eggs and whatever else was in the fridge, like diced potatoes, onion, peppers, etc. They loved it, and the evening before our wedding he fixed "glop" for all six of our kids.

Eventually Gordon dissolved his company and moved to San Antonio where his mother Annabelle and step-father Carl still lived. He was hired in the early 80's as a draftsman by Southwest Research Institute, a large not-for-profit research and development company, the same company that had hired me in 1977. I had been divorced in 1978. He was assigned to my department, so I met him on his first day of work. I was immediately attracted to him, but he was married to Carol. That marriage fell apart, and a couple of years later we started dating. We married in 1984 and moved into his small mobile home on fifteen acres of land about 30 minutes southwest of San Antonio. We wanted to build a house on our land so we sent for some basic plans. Gordon did all of the design changes and beautiful plan drawings. We moved into our new house in 1988.

When we sold our home twenty-three years later, we still had the plans, and I left them on the kitchen counter for the new owners.

As an example of his wit and independence, several years after we were married, he cut his leg badly while using a circle saw. I wasn't home at the time so he wrapped a clean dishtowel around his leg and drove to the emergency room where they stitched up his leg and gave him antibiotics. Several days later on the way home from work, he asked if we could stop at a drugstore so he could buy a cane. I asked him why he needed a cane, and he said his leg hurt. When we got home, I immediately looked at his wound. It was infected. We went to the emergency room and they admitted him to the hospital and put him on IV antibiotics for several days. When I asked him why he wanted to buy a cane instead of going to the doctor, he replied, "I had the emPHASIS on the wrong syLLABLE."

A Note to My Readers

D EMENTIA IS NOT PART of normal aging. Any type of dementia is devastating to the person afflicted and to their families. Some people live only a few years after diagnosis, but others can live fifteen years or longer. The progression is different for each person, depending on the type of dementia they have and their general health and lifestyle. Age is the number one risk factor for developing dementia, but some people, like Gordon's mother, live to a very old age and are never afflicted. By age sixty-five one in ten people will have some type of dementia, and by age eighty-five more than thirty percent will have developed dementia. Others are not so fortunate and are diagnosed in their early 40's. Early onset dementia is particularly heartbreaking and financially devastating. People are cut down in the prime of their lives and are no longer able to work. A type of Alzheimer's is familial, and can be passed down to some, but not all, members of the same family. There is a blood test available to determine if you have inherited the ApoE4 gene, but this gene is only responsible for a small percentage of all Alzheimer's cases. If you have the ApoE4 gene you have a fifty percent chance of developing Alzheimer's. Any type of dementia is very capricious and can strike without regard to age, health or income level. So far there is generally no known cause and no effective treatment and no cure. However, much research is being done worldwide and it is my hope that treatment and a cure will be found in my grandchildren's lifetime.

If your loved one develops dementia, life goes on and taking care of your loved one can be an enriching experience. After the initial shock, it is best if you can accept their diagnosis and vow to do your very best providing care and love and affection to your loved one. This is not easy; we tend to think that no one can care for our loved one like we can. This was initially my feeling, but I discovered that while no one else can love like you can, there are caregivers who can care for your loved one better than you can. It can be challenging to find the caregiver who is right for you and your loved one. You will probably have several caregivers, as I did, over the course of the illness. I was fortunate to have long-term care insurance which allowed me to keep Gordon home for the duration of most of his illness. It was my goal to have him at home until he died, but upon the advice of his doctor I placed him in a memory care facility for the last couple of months of his life. It had become an increasing challenge to find an appropriate caregiver, and I could no longer care for him by myself at home.

It is a heart-breaking decision to place your loved one in a facility. I visited several facilities and paid particular attention to how I felt when I visited. Did the atmosphere seem homey and warm, with residents engaged to the best of their abilities, in activities that stimulated them, or were they just sitting around a big room sleeping in chairs with their heads down? Are the caregivers warm and attentive and engaging the patients with music, games or conversation or are they clustered together in the kitchen or nurses station talking among themselves and all but ignoring the patients? Does the facility smell clean? I visited one facility and immediately noticed the smell of urine, but the administrator told me that it was impossible to completely eliminate the urine smell. I never went back. How is the facility set up? The one I chose had rooms down wide, fairly short hallways arranged around a large family room/dining room/kitchen. It looked and felt like a home. Some facilities have different "neighborhoods," with each neighborhood decorated and named differently. If your loved one has a tendency to wander, make sure the facility is secure so they cannot "escape."

I continued to monitor and order Gordon's medications, because I didn't want him to take anything I had not researched or had prior knowledge about. When he was in a facility, I occasionally took his laundry home and did it myself. This helped me feel like I was still doing something for him and I found out a lot about his care by doing his laundry from time to time. At the first facility he lived in, his pants, socks and shoes were wet with urine. On one visit when I patted Gordon's behind, I could feel that he didn't have any briefs on. The caregivers never mentioned this to me.

You need to be the advocate for your loved one, both at home, at the doctor's office and particularly if they are in a memory care facility. I know all of this is overwhelming and involves a lot of advance planning on your part. I think the three most important things you can do for your loved one and yourself, is **get educated, get support and get help**. I read many books and articles about this disease, a list of which is provided at the end of this book. Yes, you may find out things you really don't want to know about dementia, but I took it one day at a time and concentrated on the particular stage or problem I was having at the time. Don't try to absorb all the information at once; it can be overwhelming. Your local Alzheimer's Association will be an invaluable source of information and support. I joined a support group and after training by the Alzheimer's Association in San Antonio on facilitating support groups, I started one in the small town where I lived. Caregivers are hungry to talk about their loved ones with someone who is going through the same things they are. Many caregivers say, "I thought I was the only one going through this and it is so helpful to talk to others and discover that I am not alone on this journey."

You must get help on this journey. It is vital to maintain your health and sanity, for if you get sick, who will care for your loved one? I had help from neighbors, church friends and others, along with professional caregivers. Our families did not live near us but provided long distance support, and when I placed Gordon in the first memory care facility, both of his sons came to San Antonio and helped me. I couldn't have done it without them. But people won't know you need help unless you ask. Be specific in your requests so they will know what is expected. Gordon went to visit our neighbor across the street occasionally and they watched TV together. This man always had coffee and maybe a plate of brownies, which Gordon loved! This help enabled me to get away for a couple of hours. Another male friend came to our house and spent time with Gordon while I attended lifetime learning classes at our local library. Respite care in a secure memory care facility for Gordon was helpful when I was gone for several days visiting out-of-state family. I still worried about him, but at least I knew he was being taken care of in a safe place. It does take time and effort to arrange for respite care, and it is not without its problems, but it did enable me to get away for a few days.

While I had days of sadness and despair, I had more days of joy and happiness in caring for Gordon. I felt honored to care for him. We found humor in a lot of situations and shared many good laughs, which lifted our spirits. When I remember Gordon now, I remember him as the loving, witty man he was before dementia. I completed our journey together and did the best I knew how.

You can do the same.

RESOURCES

Recommended Reading

The Alzheimer's Journey: A Practical Perspective for Caregivers by Barbara Michels. New Mexico Chapter of the Alzheimer's Association

The Best Friends Approach to Alzheimer's Care by Virginia Bell and David Troxel

Circles of Care, How to Set Up Quality Home Care for our Elders by Ann Cason, Foreword by Reeve Lindbergh

Daily Comforts for Caregivers by Pat Samples

Don't Leave Momma Home With the Dog: Why Caregivers Do What they Do by Jo Huey

Coping with Alzheimer's: A Caregiver's Emotional Survival Guide by Rose Oliver, PhD and Frances A. Bock, PhD

Help! What Do I Do Now? Caring for Your Loved One with Alzheimer's by Nancy Nicholson

Keeping Busy: A Handbook of Activities for Persons with Dementia by James R. Dowling, Foreword by Nancy L. Mace

Kisses for Elizabeth: Common Sense Guidelines for Alzheimer's and Dementia Care by Stephanie D. Zeman, MSN, RN

Lewy Body Dementia: A Caregiver's Guide, by Helen Buell Whitworth and James Whitworth

On Pluto: Inside the Mind of Alzheimer's by Greg O'Brien

Slow Dancing with a Stranger: Lost and Found in the Age of Alzheimer's by Meryl Comer

The 36-Hour Day: A Family Guide to Caring for Persons with Alzheimer's Disease, Related Dementing Illnesses, and Memory Loss in Later Life by Nancy L. Mace, M.A. and Peter V. Rabins, MD, MPH

The Theft of Memory: Losing My Father One Day at a Time by Jonathan Kozol, MD

Untangling Alzheimer's: The Guide for Families and Professionals by Tam Cummings, PhD

Recommended Websites

www.AARP.org/caregiving ~ Caregiving basics, personal stories, online community and general support via AARP.

www.Caregiver.com ~ Publishers of *Today's Caregiver* magazine.

www.Caregiver.org ~ Family Caregiver Alliance® at the National Center on Caregiving serves as a public voice for caregivers, shining light on daily challenges faced by caregivers and championing their cause through education, services, and advocacy.

www.CaregiverAction.org ~ Caregiver Action Network (CAN) is a national organization working to improve the quality of life for the more than 90 million caregivers in the United States.

www.DailyCaring.com ~ Practical tips, advice, personal stories, and resources related to caregiving and aging, boiled down to the essential, useful and actionable information.

www.DementiaCareCentral.com ~ A well-organized online resource center for dementia caregivers.

www.TamCummings.com ~ Tam Cummings, PhD, is a gerontologist dedicated to untangling the complexities of dementia. She is the author of *Untangling Alzheimer's*.

www.TeepaSnow.com ~ Teepa Snow is one of the leading educators on dementia and its care in the United States and Canada.

Ruth and Gordon Pollard, March 31, 1984, with their children,
Steven, Brian and Jeffrey Pilgrim and Tammy, Tim and John Pollard

About the Author

Ruth baird pollard kept a journal during most of the six and a half years she was a caregiver for her husband, Gordon, from diagnosis in 2007 until his death in 2012. Her intimate writings were later edited and published as *Loving Gordon: A Dementia Caregiver's Journey*. She has an Associate's Degree in Business Technology from San Antonio College in San Antonio, Texas. She also has taken many writing courses and is a member of SouthWest Writers.

An active volunteer with the local Alzheimer's Association, Pollard is a facilitator for two support groups where she helps other caregivers along their journeys. She has five sons, five daughters-in-law, nine grandchildren, and four great-grandchildren. She lives in Albuquerque, New Mexico, with her faithful companion, Maggie the cat.

For author inquiries and speaking engagement requests, visit www.TheCaregiversJourney.com.

Publisher's Note

Thank you for reading Ruth Baird Pollard's
Loving Gordon: A Dementia Caregiver's Journey.

If you enjoyed this book, kindly support the author by helping
others find it. Here are some suggestions for your consideration:

- Write an online customer review wherever books are sold

- Gift this book to family and friends
  who will benefit from its message

- Share a photo of the book on social media and tag
  #RuthPollard and #LovingGordon

- Bring in Ruth Pollard as a speaker
  for your club or organization

- Suggest *Loving Gordon* to your local book club

- For ordering inquiries, contact Citrine Publishing at
  (828) 585-7030 or Publisher@CitrinePublishing.com

- Meet Ruth Pollard and connect with her at
  www.TheCaregiversJourney.com